ENCYCLOPAEDIA OF INDIAN GOVERNMENT: PROGRAMMES AND POLICIES

ENCYCLOPAEDIA
OF
INDIAN GOVERNMENT:
PROGRAMMES AND POLICIES

Vol. 32

Food and Consumer Affairs

Edited by

Satish Tiwari

ANMOL PUBLICATIONS PVT. LTD.

NEW DELHI - 110 002 (INDIA)

ANMOL PUBLICATIONS PVT. LTD.
4374/4B, Ansari Road, Daryaganj
New Delhi - 110 002

Encyclopaedia of Indian Government: Programmes and Policies

First Edition, 2000

ISBN 81-261-0515-1 (Set)

PRINTED IN INDIA

Published by J.L. Kumar for Anmol Publications Pvt. Ltd., New Delhi - 110 002 and Printed at Mehra Offset Press, Delhi.

Contents

Preface

Encyclopaedia of Indian Government: Programmes and Policies contains authoritative information on about fifty departmental policies and their future developmental programmes.

Organised to be completed in 40 volumes, this gigantic work covers Agriculture; Atomic Energy; Chemicals and Fertilizers; Coal; Commerce; Communication; Culture; Defence; Education; Environment and Forests; External Affairs; Finance; Food & Consumer Affairs; Food Processing Industries; Health and Family Welfare; Home Affairs and Internal Security; Human Resources; Industry; Information and Broadcasting; Labour; Law, Justice and Company Affairs; Non-conventional Energy Sources; Ocean Development; Parliamentary Affairs; Personnel, Public Grievances and Pensions; Petroleum and Natural Gas; Planning and Programme Implementation; Planning and Statistics; Posts and Telegraphs; Power; Rural Development; Science and Technology; Social Justice and Empowerment; Space; States Affairs; Steel; Steel and Mines; Sugar and Edible Oils; Surface Transport; Textiles; Tourism; Urban Development; Water Resources; Women and Child development etc.

Based on the information derived from authoritative sources, this work contains authentic facts and figures. I am deeply beholden to all the scholars whose writings are cited or substantially made use of in the present work. I am also thankful to Anmol Publications Pvt. Ltd. for undertaking publication of this encyclopaedia. I am solely responsible for shortcomings in presentation of matter.

Encyclopaedic in nature, this will prove a dependable reference work for scholars and academics besides those appearing for different competitive examinations.

—**Satish Tiwari**

1

Introduction

The Ministry of Food consisting of the Department of Food and the Department of Food Procurement and Distribution and the Ministry of Civil Supplies, Consumer Affairs and Public Distribution were merged with effect from 4.6.1997 to form a new Ministry viz. the Ministry of Food and Consumer Affairs consisting of the following three Departments:-

1. Department of Food & Civil Supplies;
2. Department of Sugar and Edible Oils; and
3. Department of Consumer Affairs.

This Annual Report is in respect of Department of Food and Civil Supplies and the Department of Sugar and Edible Oils while the Department of Consumer Affairs are bringing out a separate Annual Report for that Department.

Department of food and civil supplies

The Department of Food & Civil Supplies is charged with the prime responsibility of the management of the food economy of the country. The twin objectives of the Department are to ensure remunerative rates for our farmers and the foodgrains at reasonable prices to the consumers through the public distribution system. The Department is concerned with the formulation of policies concerning the foodgrains sector and is also responsible for the development aspects of the foodgrains, its storage, acquisition and the construction of godowns for foodgrains. The Department is also concerned with the International Conferences, Associations and other Bodies concerning food and for entering into treaties and agreements with foreign countries and implementing treaties, agreements and conventions with foreign countries relating to trade and commerce in foodgrains and other foodstuffs.

The Department of Food & Civil Supplies is responsible for implementation of the scheme of minimum support price to the producers of wheat, paddy and coarsegrains and the distribution of foodgrains from the Central Pool. With a view to ensuring food security, activities such as procurement of foodgrains, building up and maintenance of food stocks, their quality, storage, movement and delivery to the distributing agencies are undertaken. A close watch is kept on the stock and price levels of foodgrains and efforts are made to ensure their adequate availability at reasonable prices in different parts of the country.

Procurment

In keeping with the national policy of providing price support to the major foodgrains of the country viz. wheat, paddy and coarsegrains, the Government continued to procure foodgrains conforming to prescribed specifications offered by the farmers at the notified Minimum Support Prices (MSP). The price support operations for wheat and paddy are undertaken by the Food Corporation of India in association with the State agencies. For the 1998-99 Kharif Marketing Season, MSP of paddy was raised by Rs. 25/- per quintal for the common variety and Grade 'A' as compared to the MSP of previous season. Similarly the MSP for wheat was raised by Rs. 40/- per quintal for the 1998-99 Rabi

Marketing Season. The Comparative Minimum Support Prices of wheat and paddy for the 1997-98 and 1998-99 seasons are given below:-

(Price in Rs. per quintal)

	Wheat	*Paddy*	
		Common	*Grade 'A'*
1997-98	415	415	445
1998-99	455	440	470

A proposal to implement the scheme of decentralised procurement of foodgrains in the States of Uttar Pradesh, Madhya Pradesh, Rajasthan and Bihar is under consideration of the Government. The Government of West Bengal has been undertaking procurment of rice under the said scheme from Kharif Marketing Season 1997-98. A decision has been taken to implement the Scheme in respect of the States of Uttar Pradesh and Madhya Pradesh from the Rabi and Kharif Marketing Season 1999-2000.

Beside's extending price support to farmers for wheat and paddy, rice was also procured under levy from rice millers/dealers at the prices fixed separately for each State.

The procurement of rice for the Central Pool (including paddy in terms of rice) during 199798 Kharif Marketing Season (October 1997 - September, 1998) was 14.31 million tonnes as against 12.22 million tonnes procured during the previous season. A quantity of 5.49. million tonnes of rice was procured as on 22.12.98 for Central Pool during the current 1998-99 Kharif Marketing Season. Procurment of rice is in progress and is likely to be in the range of 11 to 12 Million Tonnes.

The wheat procurement during 1997-98 Rabi Marketing Season was 9.30 million tonnes as against 8.16

million tonnes during 1996-97 season. In the 1998-99 Rabi Marketing Season 12-65 million tonnes of wheat was procured for Central Pool.

From the 1990-91 Rabi Marketing Season, FCI became the nodal agency for the procurement of Rabi and Kharif coarsegrains throughout the country. The Minimum Support Price of coarsegrains viz. jowar, bajra, ragi and maize was fixed at Rs. 390/- per quintal and for barley at Rs. 350/- per quintal for 1998-99 Kharif/Rabi Marketing Season over the procurement price of Rs. 360/- per quintal for jowar, bajra ragi, and maize and Rs. 305/- per quintal for barley in 1997-98 Kharif/Rabi Marketing Season. However, as the prevailing open market prices of coarsegrains were generally much higher than the Minimum Support Price, the procurement of coarsegrains has been negligible.

It has been the policy of Government of India to treat the entire country as a single food zone. Free movement of wheat, wheat products, coarsegrains and levy-free rice is permissible throughout the country.

Central issue prices

Consequent upon the decision of the Central Government to streamline and restructure PDS with focus on the poor (the Targeted PDS), the CIP (Ex-FCI godowns) of wheat and rice issued from Central Pool were revised from Ist June, 1997.

The CIP of wheat are Rs. 250/- per quintal for BPL and Rs. 450/- per quintal for APL w.e.f. 1.6.1997. The CIP of wheat for APL has however been revised to Rs. 650/- per quintal w.e.f. 29.1.1999. The CIPs of rice are Rs. 350/- per quintal for common and Grade 'A' for BPL category, and Rs. 700/- per quintal for Grade'A' for APL category w.e.f. 1.12.1997. The CIP of grade'A' rice for APL has been revised to Rs. 905/- per quintal w.e.f. 29.1.1999. The CIP of common rice was fixed at Rs. 550/ per quintal from 1.12.1997 for APL families in J&K, Himachal Pradesh and hilly areas of North Eastern States (including Sikkim and U.P.) which has been revised to Rs. 700/- per quintal w.e.f 29.1.1999.

The CIP for coarsegrains was fixed at Rs. 199/- per quintal for PDS and Rs. 149/- per quintal for RPDS w.e.f. Ist October, 1990. Central Issue Prices (CIP) of coarsegrains have remained unchanged ever since.

Regulation of foodgrains trade

The policy of deregulating the foodgrains trade in the country has been consistently followed till the rabi crop of 1995-96 when the procurement did not come upto the expected level combined with the decline in the production of wheat. Taking advantage of this situation, the traders in several parts of the country then resorted to unethical trade practices like hoarding and black marketing. Thus, with a view to checking the rise in the prices of wheat and wheat products in market, a decision was taken in December, 1996 to reintroduce licensing and stock limits on wheat. This policy is still continuing.

Keeping in view the depleted stock level of rice ii the Central Pool the Government of India has not agreed to grant exemption to any variety of non-basmati rice, either for internal market or for export from levy obligation in the Kharif Marketing Season 1996-97. The State Governments/ UT Administrations have been requested to ensure that the Statutory Levy Orders are implemented effectively and into without any exemption in the 1996-97 Kharif Marketing Season. This policy continued during the 1961798 Kharif Marketing Season. The same policy is being adopted during the current Kharif Marketing Season 1998-99 also. However, on account of rains and severe damage to crops, on the requests of the Governments of Punjab and Haryana, they were allowed to exempt the rice millers of their States from levy on the paddy procured by them upto 10-10-1998 and

31-10-1998 respectively during the current Kharif Marketing Season.

Stock of foodgrains

The stocks of rice and wheat in the Central Pool as on 1.10.98 stood at 8.96 million tonnes and 15.24 million tonnes respectively, as against the buffer stocking norms of 6.00 million tonnes of rice and 10.60 million tonnes of wheat.

The Government reviews, I on a monthly basis, the position of foodgrains stocks held in the Central Pool by the FCI and the State Governments and their agencies. The Stock of rice and wheat in the Central Pool by and large remained satisfactory.

R&D efforts

During the year 1997-98 IGMRI, Hapur and its Field Stations undertook a two year project to estimate the quantitative losses in Wheat during different post-harvest operations viz. harvesting, threshing, transportation, processing and storage at farm level. The same is in various stages of progress.

During the year 1997-98, a four-member team of Steering Committee on Automation of Mechanised Handling and Bulk Storage of Foodgrains visited China, Philippines and Australia to study the prevalent practices there in order to explore the feasibility of their introduction in our country.

Storage

The Food Corporation of India, Central Warehousing Corporation and State Warehousing Corporations have together constructed additional storage capacity of 3.48 lakh tonnes during 199798. An additional storage capacity of 3.89 lakh tonnes is expected to be constructed by these three agencies during the year 1998-99.

Movement

Improvement in availability of foodgrains in various States and reduction in off-take during April-July, 1998 resulted in reduction in sponsored foodgrains movement by the Food Corporation of India during April-December, 1998. The overall movement during 1998-99 is expected to be about 17.5 million tonnes as against 19.0 million tonnes during the previous year. Import of wheat also led to reduction in movement ex-North and the average number of foodgrains rakes moving ex-North during 1998-99 is estimated to be 13 per day as against 14.4 rakes per day during 1997-98.

Induction of foodgrains to the North Eastern Region considerably improved during 1998-99 but the stock level as on 1st December, 1998 reduced to about 1.47 lakh MTs as against 1.54 lakh MTs as on 1st April, 1998 due to increase in offtake of foodgrains in the NE Region, natural calamities, incessant rains, floods, other operational problems and capacity constraints. Efforts are being made to build up the stock levels.

Winter stocking of Leh and Kargil areas was completed much in advance of the onset of winter. Movement of the gift consignment of about 20,000 MTs of par boiled rice from the Government of India to the Government of Bangladesh was organised by rail at short notice during October-December, 1998.

2

Highlights

Price trend and availability of essential commodities

During the first 9 months (April-December, 98) of the current financial year 1998-99, the rate of inflation based on Wholesale Price Index (WPI) numbers has recorded an increase of 5.8% as against a low rise of 4.3% in the corresponding period of the last year. Though the prices of most of the essential commodities were ruling at a reasonable level, an abnormal increase was noted in the prices of some food items such as vegetables, pulses and edible oils. Among the three, major groups, the WPI of primary articles rose at a higher rate of 12.2% while the price indices of manufactured products increased only by 3.3% and that of fuel, power, light and lubricants observed a negative growth rate of 0.5% during this period. Among individual items, the price indices of rice, wheat, arhar, moong, masur, urad, potato, onions, chillies, atta, mustard oil and groundnut oil rose by a higher margin as compared to a modest increase in the case of jowar, bajra, milk, mutton, sugar, salt, vanaspati, coconut oil and cotton cloth during the period April-December, 98. A decline was noted in the WPI of gram, fish, tea, gur and kerosene during the same period.

The higher increase in the prices of some commodities are mainly attributed to gap in their demand and supply, fall in production, unfavourable weather conditions coupled with unseasonal rains resulting in damage to crops, increase in the cost of inputs and other seasonal factors.

As in the past years, the major thrust of the Government policy has been to enhance the indigenous production of essential commodities and to ensure their easy availability to the common man at reasonable prices throughout the year. In order to supplement the availability in the market, imports are allowed in the case of pulses, edible oils, onions etc. The import of onions has been placed under OGL with zero import duty. The customs duty on import of edible oils under OGL has been reduced from 25% to 15% with effect from 10.7.98. The 4% special additional import duty on edible oils used in vanaspati has been abolished with effect from 31.10.98. State/ UT Governments have been advised to take stringent actions against hoarders, black marketers etc. under the Essential Commodities Act and the Prevention of Blackmarketing and Maintenance of Supplies of Essential Commodities Act. In order to reduce the pressure on the prices, onion was sold through Public Distribution agencies at a subsidised rate of Rs. 10 per kg. in Delhi with effect from 14.7.98 till 31.12.98. A meeting of the Chief Secretaries of State Govts./UTs was convened by the Cabinet Secretary on 7.11.98 to discuss the issue of price rise and measures to control the prices. The Prime Minister had convened a meeting of all Chief Ministers of States/UTs on 27.11.98 to review the situation arising out of abnormal increase in the prices of essential commodities witnessed during the second half of 1999. The decisions taken during the course of discussions held in the meeting are being implemented, including setting up of Price Monitoring Cell in the Department of Consumer Affairs, National Crop Forecasting Centre in the Department of Agriculture & Cooperation, restructuring of Cabinet Committee on Prices (CCP) and reconstituting Special Action

Committee of Secretaries on monitoring of prices (SACP) into High Powered Price Monitoring Board (HPPMB).

Consumer protection programme

The Department continued with the monitoring of functioning of the consumer courts set up under the Consumer Protection Act,. 1986 and took remedial measures to remove the problems faced by them.

To strengthen the infrastructure of consumer courts in the States, a scheme of one-time financial assistance of Rs. 61 crores was initiated in 1995-96 with the approval of Planning Commission to supplement the effort of the States/ UT Administrations. Four instalments of the grant amounting Rs. 58.12 crores were released during 95-98.

The 19th meeting of the Central Consumer Protection Council (CCPC) was held on October 18, 1998.

A permanent Standing Working Group has been set up under the aegis of the Council to review/monitor the recommendations of CCPC. The second meeting of the working Group was held on 29.4.1998.

To generate consumer awareness, , the Department has produced 12-episode programme on consumer protection in collaboration with Doordarshan, entitled "GRAHAK DOST" which were telecast during June-September, 1998.

The Department continued with the release of grant to non-governmental organisations from the Consumer Welfare Fund. 'Me main objective of the Fund is to provide financial assistance to promote the welfare of consumers.

A ten-minute weekly programme "APNE ADHIKAR" on consumer protection has been on the air in regional languages from various commercial broadcasting stations of AIR since December, 1997.

The Department has decided to set up Consumer Information Centres one in each State to begin with. These Centres will function as library, information, guidance, research and testing centres. These Centres will be manned by reputed NGOs financed under the Consumer Welfare Fund.

Consumer Cooperatives

The Consumer Cooperatives are playing an important role in providing essential and other commodities to the consumers at reasonable prices. The Consumer Cooperatives have continued to help in strengthening the distributive network of essential commodities and stabilizing the price line to the extent possible for protecting the interests of the consumers against artificial scarcity, over-charging of prices, supply of sub-standard goods as also unfair trade practices resorted to by the private trade. The democratically elected managements of consumer cooperatives also help these organisations to gain better acceptance with the consumers. As per the available information, out of the total number of 4,49,469 fair price shops functioning in the country upto December, 1997, 94,124 were in the cooperative sector (roughly about 20.94%). Out of these, number of shops being run by the cooperatives in the rural and urban areas were 74,789 (79.45%) and 19,335 (20.54%) respectively.

It has been the policy of the Govt. of India to encourage the development of consumer cooperatives, so as to protect the interests of the common consumers in the country.

Forward trading

The Department administers the Forward Contracts (Regulation) Act, 1952 which provides for the regulation of matters relating to forward contracts, prohibition of options in goods and the matters connected therewith. The Forward Markets Commission is a statutory body established under this Act. Its functions have been listed in the Act, the important ones being to advise the Central Government in respect of recognition or withdrawal of recognition of any association and in respect of matters arising out of the administration of the Act, to keep forward markets under observation and to take appropriate action in relation to them and to make recommendations to improve the organisation and working of forwarding contracts etc.

At present, futures trading is regulated through 15 recognized associations in eight commodities viz. castor seed, pepper, turmeric, potatoes, gur, hessian, jute goods and cotton. Futures trading in cotton has commenced in December, 1998. Besides, Government have permitted futures trading in coffee at the Coffee Futures Exchange India Ltd, Bangalore. The Soyabean Processors Association of India has been selected for futures contracts in soyabean, its oil and oil cake. International futures contracts in pepper have started since November, 1997. The Government's decision to set up an International Futures Exchange in castor oil is also under implementation. Govt. have permitted dollar denominated futures contracts in both pepper and castor oil.

Bureau of Indian standards

The Bureau of Indian Standards has made steady progress in various fields of its activities, namely, standards formulation, product and system certification schemes. BIS has formulated national Standards on Environmental 'Management Systems based on ISO 14000 series of standards.

The Environmental Management System Certification Scheme was launched for units which have commitment environmental protection and greener technologies. The first licence has been issued to a cement unit under this scheme.

Keeping in view the international requirement for safety of food products to Hazard Analysis and Critical Control I'd (HACCP) Certification, BIS has formulated IS: 150(standard which is based on Codex Alementarius Commission(document ALINORM 97/13A. BIS has launched HACCP(certification scheme in 1998 and granted first licence to 0 Mother Dairy under ISO 9000 - HACCP (Hazard Analysis Critical Control Points) certification. Apart from Moth Dairy four more licences have been granted under this scheme

Weights and measures

Weights and Measures Laws form the basis c commercial transaction in any civilized society. To ensure accuracy of measurement in such transaction, the Government has enacted two legislations namely, the Standards of Weigh and Measures Act, 1976 and the Standards of Weights an Measures (Enforcement) Act, 1985. A National Forum a Legal Metrology has been constituted by the Department to advise it on policy matters relating to weights and measures An Expert Group constituted by the Government to review various legislations administered by the Department has submitted its recommendations for amending certain provisions of the Weights and Measures Acts and their recommendation is under consideration.

The Standards of Weights and Measures (Packaged Commodities) Rules, 1977 regulate pre-packed commodities sold in the course of commercial transaction. The Rules require importers to indicate some declarations on imported packaged commodities in the interest of the consumers. The Rules are reviewed from time to time in consultation with the industry trade and consumer organizations to make it more practical and in keeping with the development in the field.

The Department has already set in motion the process of adopting new specifications in the Standards of Weights and Measures (General) Rules, 1981 in accordance with the recommendations made by the International Organization of Legal Metrology (OIML) Towards this end, the Rules have been amended revising the specifications of non-automatic weighing instruments based on OIML recommendations. Adoption of the new specifications would help the Indian industries to compete in the international market.

During the 9th Five Year Plan period, the Ministry has undertaken schemes to establish Regional Reference Standards Laboratories (RRSL) for the northern and the north eastern regions and to construct a laboratory building for the RRSL at Bhubaneswar. The existing laboratories at Ahmedabad and Bangalore are also being modernized to meet the requirements of the industry.

3

Food Processing Industries

The Ministry of Food Processing Industries was set up in July, 1988 to give an impetus to the development-of food processing industries in the country. A strong and effective food processing sector plays a significant role in diversification and commercialisation of agriculture, improves value addition of the agricultural produce, generates employment, enhances income of farmers and creates surplus for export of agro foods. The Ministry of Food Processing Industries is concerned with the formulation and implementation of the policies and plans for the food processing industries within the overall national priorities and objectives

Allocation of business

A. The subjects allocated to the Ministry are as under:-

1. Fruit and vegetable processing industry (including freezing and dehydration).
2. Foodgrain milling industry.
3. Dairy products such As milk powder, infant milk food, malted food, condensed milk, ghee etc.
4. Processing and referigeration of poultry and eggs, meat & meat products.
5. Processing of fish (including canning and freezing).
6. Planning, development and control of, and

assistance to industries relating to bread, oilseeds, meals (edible), breakfast foods, biscuits, confectionery (including cocoa processing and chocolate making), malt extract, protein isolate, high protein food, weaning food and extruded food products (including other ready-to-eat foods).

7. Beer, including nonalcoholic beer.
8. Alcoholic drinks from non-molasses base.
9. Aerated waters/soft drinks and other processed foods.
10. Specialised packaging for food processing industries.
11. Establishment and servicing of the Development Councils for food processing industries.
12. Technical assistance and advice to food processing industry.

Goals & objectives

The Ministry of Food Processing Industries is the nodal agency of the Government of India for processed foods and is responsible for developing a strong and vibrant food processing sector with emphasis on the following --

— Stimulating demand for appropriate processed foods.

— Achieving maximum value addition and by-product utilisation

— Creating increased job opportunities particularly in rural areas.

— Enabling fanners to reap the benefits of modem technology.

— Creating surpluses for exports.

In the era of economic liberalisation where the private, public and co-operative sectors are to play their rightful role in development of food processing sector, the Ministry acts as a catalyst for bringing in greater investment into this sector, guiding and helping the industry in a proper direction, encouraging exports and creating a conducive environment for healthy growth of the food processing industry. Within this overall objective, the Ministry aims at :

— Better utilisation and value addition of agricultural produce for enhancement of income of farmers.

— Minimising wastage at all stages in the food processing chain by the development of infrastructure for storage, transportation and processing of agro-food produce.

— Induction of modern technology into the food processing industries from both domestic and external sources.

— Maximum utilisation of agricultural residues and by-products of the primary agricultural produce as also of the processed food industry.

— To encourage R&D in food processing for product and process development and improved packaging.

— To provide policy support, promotional initiatives and physical facilities to promote value added exports.

Role of the ministry

The functions of the Ministry can be broadly classified as follows

1. *Policy support*

   a) Formulation and implementation of policies for food processing industries within overall national priorities and objectives

b) Facilitating the creation of a conducive policy environment for healthy growth of the food processing sector.

c) Promoting rationalisation of tariffs and duties relating to food processing sector.

2. *Developmental*

a) Assistance under various plan schemes

b) Widening the R&D base in food processing by involvement of various R&D institutes and support to various R&D activities relating to development of product, process and packaging with special emphasis on traditional technologies.

c) Human Resource Development both for entrepreneurs as well as the workers engaged in the food processing industry by upgradation of their skills.

d) Assistance for setting up analytical and testing laboratories, active participation in the laying down of food standards as well as their harmonisation with international standards.

3. *Promotional*

Assistance for organisation of workshops, seminars, exhibitions and fairs etc.,

b) Assistance for studies/surveys etc.,

c) Publications and films.

4. *Regulatory*

Implementation of Fruit Products Order (FPO).

Staff strength

The total sanctioned strength of the Ministry as on 31.12.1998 is as follows:

Group of Posts	*No. of sanctioned posts*	*No. of posts held by*	
		SCs	*STs*
Group A	31	3	-
Group B	45	8	3
Group C	51	6	2
Group D	20	6	-
Total	147	23	5

Directorate of F&VP

The regulatory functions are carried out at the Ministry level and also through the Directorate of Fruit and Vegetable Preservation (F&VP).

The Directorate of F&VP has four regional offices at Delhi. Calcutta. Madras and Mumbai headed by Deputy Directors and also has two sub-offices at Licknow and Guwahati under the administration control the regional offices at Delhi and Calcutta respectively.

Paddy processing research centre

The Paddy Processing Research Centre at Thanjavur is ail autonomous body under the administrative control of the Ministry. This Centre was Set up in December, 1984 as a Society registered under the Tamil Nadu Societies Act. The centre carries Out basic research work oil different applied aspects of rice processing and by-product utilisation like drying, storage, parboiling, milling, bran stabilisation and oil extraction etc. The Centre is fully funded by this Ministry.

Interface with other agencies

For achieving its objectives, the Ministry, apart from various Ministries of the Government of India like Agriculture, Industry, Commerce and Health interacts with various State Governments through their

Departments/Ministry of Food Processing Industries or nominated nodal agencies which are responsible for implementing programmes relating to this sector in the concerned State Governments. The Ministry also interacts with various promotional organisations like Agricultural Products Export Development Authority (APEDA), Marine Products Export Development Authority (MPEDA), National Research Development Corporation (NRDC), National Co-operative Development Corporation (NCDC), National Horticulture Board, various R&D institutes and Quality Control Laboratories and various Industries Associations.

Recent initiatives

The Processed Food Sector had been facing serious problems in financing the projects as the food processing industries are high risk prone with long gestation period and the returns are small. As a result, the projects in this sector were not finding favourable consideration by the financial institutions. Considering the demand of the industry and in view of the vast potential of the growth of the agro-processing sector, the Government has now decided to include agro processing sector within the definition of "Priority Sector" for bank lending.

Expansion of the role of regional offices of directorate of fruits & vegetable preservation

In view of the liberalized economic scenario, the role of regional offices of the Directorate of Fruit and Vegetable Preservation under the Ministry has been expanded. These offices will henceforth act as a link between the Ministry and the State Nodal Agencies, disseminate information on the plan schemes and programmes of the Ministry, monitor the projects assisted by the Ministry, provide technical guidance to the entrepreneurs and provide technical help to the Food Processing and Training Centres funded by the Ministry.

Interaction with state nodal agencies

Most of the States & Union Territories, except for West Bengal, do not have a separate department for the processed food sector. Ministry ill Consultation with the state Governments has nominated a State Nodal Agency in each State/Union Territory for coordinating all efforts towards development of food processing sector. A conference of the State Nodal Agencies was held on 11.1.99 at New Delhi. The conference provided useful feedback oil problems faced by State Nodal Agencies and identifying areas for development of this sector.

Investments

In the era of economic liberalisation where the private, public and cooperative sectors are to play their rightful role in development of food processing industries, Ministry acts as a catalyst for bringing in greater investments into this sector.

Since August 1991 till December 1998, 4676 Industrial Entrepreneur Memorandas (IEMs) envisaging ail investment of Rs.53490 crores and direct employment of approximately 7.40 lakh persons have been received for various sectors of food processing. Out of the IEMs filed during this period, 3999 IEMs envisaging ail investment of Rs.46924 crores and direct employment of approximately 6.73 lakh persons are for non-urban areas. About 39% of these investments are for backward areas. Of these, 6461 EMs envisaging ail investment of approximately Rs.7375 crores and direct employment of 81686 persons have already been implemented.

During the same period, Government has also approved 1089 proposals of industrial licences and 100% export oriented units, envisaging ail investment" of over Rs. 18685 crores and direct employment of approximately 2.70 lakh persons. Out of these, 206 proposals envisaging ail investment of Rs.3,836 crores and direct employment of approximately 0.86 lakh persons have already been implemented. Out of the total proposed investment of Rs. 72175 crores, foreign investment envisaged is Rs. 8809 crores. Out of the total proposed foreign investment of Rs. 8809 crores in the food processing sectors the actual inflow till December 1998 is over Rs.1850 crores.

Growth of industry

(i) Grain processing

Due to the constant efforts made by the Ministry from time to time, the number of modern/modernised rice mills has gone up from practically nil in 1970 to 34688 as on 01.01.1999. As a result of improved availability of bran from these modern and rnodernised mills, the processing of bran is estimated to be around 33 lakh tonnes in 199899.

Thirteen Regional Extension Service Centres have been set LIP in various states with Agricultural Universities/Research institutions for propagating the benefits of modernisation of rice milling industry and by-product utilisation through organising seminars, group discussions/setting up demonstration units and preparation of technical literature etc. For Rice Mills &Allied Equipment Testing Centres set up at Tamil Nadu Agricultural University, Coimbatore; Indian Institute of Technology, Kharagpur; Harcourt Butler Technological Institute, Kanpur; and Mahatma Phule Agriculture University, Pune are continuing their activities by providing necessary assistance to machinery manufacturers and millers for testing of equipments, as well as for selection, operation and maintenance of machinery. Post-Harvest Technology Centre at Indian Institute of Technology (IIT), Kharagpur, offers training courses of long term duration leading to M.Tech, Ph.D. &

Post Doctoral Degree and also short term courses for managers/mill operators etc. The centre also undertakes research & development project as per need of the industry.

No licence is required for manufacture of wheat products. There are no controls on price and distribution of wheat products. The mills have been given a free hand to obtain their requirements of wheat from any source, thereby avoiding their dependence on government for supply of raw materials. Nearly 10.5 million tonnes of wheat is converted into various wheat products by about 820 roller flour mills in the country every year against an installed capacity of 19.5 million tonnes.

(ii) Consumer food industries

The consumer food industry mainly consists of ready-to-eat or ready-to-cook products such as pasta products, cocoa based products, bakery products, biscuits, soft drinks, etc.

a) Bakery

Bakery industry in India is probably the largest among the processed food industries, production of which has been increasing steadily in the country. The two major bakery industries, viz., bread and biscuit account for about 82% of the total bakery products. The annual production of bakery products which includes bread, biscuits, pasteries, cakes, buns, rusk, etc., most of which are in the unorganised sector, is estimated to be in excess of 30 lakh tonnes.

The production of bread and biscuits in the country, both in the organised and unorganized sectors, is estimated to be around 15 lakh tonnes and 11 lakh tonnes respectively. Of the total production of bread and biscuits, about 35% is produced in the organised sector and the remaining is manufactured in the unorganized sector.

Another wheat based product known by its generic name, pasta products, comprising of noodles, vermicelli, macaroni and spaghetti is gaining popularity.

b) Cocoa products

There are 20 units engaged in the manufacture of cocoa products like chocolates, drinking chocolates, cocoa butter, cocoa butter substitutes, cocoa based malted milk foods with a production of approximately 34 thousand tonnes.

c) Soft drinks

The production of soft drinks during the period under review has increased from 4920 million bottles in 1997-98 to 5670 million bottles during the period under review.

d) Beer & alcoholic drinks

At present, there are 36 units manufacturing beer under licence from Government of India having an estimated output of 4.33 lakh KL per annum. On the other hand, the production of alcoholic drinks from non-molasses sources is very small in the country compared to the total production of alcoholic drinks. However, with various foreign companies producing non-molasses alcoholic drinks such drinks are gaining popularity in the domestic market.

iii) Fruit & vegetable processing industries

The estimated installed capacity of fruit and vegetable processing industries has increased from 20.4 lakh tonnes in 1997 to 20.8 lakh tonnes in 1998. The production of processed fruits and vegetables in the country has increased from 9.1 lakh tonnes in 1997 to 9.4 lakh tonnes in 1998. During the same period the number of licences issued under Fruit Product Order (FPO), 1955 has increased to 5 112 from 4932.

iv) Milk & milk products

During the year 1998-99, dairying in India would achieve another milestone. With its milk production projected to be 74 million tonnes as against 71 million tonnes during 1997-98, India would become the largest milk producing country in the world.

There has been increase in the estimated production of milk powder including infant milk food from 2.15 lakh tonnes in the year 1997 to 2.22 lakh tonnes in the year 1998 and the estimated production of malted food product has increased from 55,000 tonnes in the year 1997 to 65,000 tonnes in the year 1998. The production of cheese in the organised sector in the year 1998 has been estimated as 5,000 tonnes. The estimated product ion of condensed milk has increased from 7,800 tonnes in the year 1997 to 9,000 tonnes in the year 1998.

v) Meat and poultry processing

The production of meat and meat products has shown an impressive growth. The details of production of meat and meat products from 1993 to 1997 is as under:

(Thousand Tonnes)

	1993	*1994*	*1995*	*1996*	*1997*
Mutton & goat meat	623	636	647	669	670
Pork	366	366	420	420	420
Chicken (Poultry Meat)	382	442	578	480	580
Cattle (Beef)	1215	1290	1292	1292	1292
Buffalo (Meat)	1182	1200	1204	1204	1205

vi) Fish processing

60% of the production of fish in India is from marine sources with coastal fishing constituting the bulk and only 2% comes from deep sea resources. Production of fish from both marine and inland sources has increased from 5.34 million tonnes in 1996-97 to 5.38 million tonnes in 1997-98.

The total meat production in the country is of the tune of 4.2 million tonnes per annum. The slaughtered .rate in relation to the population of animals is about 6% in the case of cattle, 10% in the case of buffalo, 99% in case of pigs, 3 1 % in case of sheep and 39% in case of goat.

Processing of marine products into canned and frozen forms is carried out almost entirely for the export Market. In all, there are 407 freezing units, 13 canning units, 154 ice-making units, 11 fish meal units and also about 489 cold storage units in this sector.

Development councils

The first meeting of the Development Council for Processed Fruits and Vegetables, Cereal Products and Beverages was held on 14th December, 1998 under the -chairmanship of Secretary, Ministry of Food Processing Industries. Following action points have been identified.

Short term:

1. A study to be undertaken to find out the implications of post-WTO regime, opportunities and challenges emerging out of it in the processed food sector and the action needed on the part of the Ministry and the Industry;
2. CFTRI to make available item specific standards of Good Manufacturing Practices (GMP) to the industry; and

3. Role of Regional offices of F&VP Directorate to be expanded to cover extension of developmental activities also. The Ministry has already taken action on this.

Long term:

A Task Force has been set up to identify the problems faced by processed food industry and to suggest short term and long term action points. Apart from other issues, the Task Force would suggest changes in export and import policy, identify items which require dereservation and suggest measures for harmonisation of food laws.

Exports

Exports of processed fruits and vegetables in 199899 is estimated to be around Rs.640 crores as against Rs.745 crores in 1997-98. Export of animal products is estimated to be around Rs.955 crores in 1998-99 as against Rs.910 crores in 1997-98. Export of processed foods (including cereal based products) is estimated to increase to Rs.6900 crores in 1998-99 from Rs.6371 crores in 1997-98 and export of marine products is expected to increase from Rs.4643 crores to Rs.6300 crores during the same period.

4

Organisational Set up

Organisation

Shri S.S. Barnala, Minister for Chemicals and Fertilisers assumed additional charge of Ministry of Food and Consumer Affairs with effect from 19.3.1998 and continued to hold the additional charge during 1998-99. Shri Satyapal Singh Yadav continued to hold the charge of Minister of State (Food & Consumer Affairs) during 1998-99. Shri R.S. Mathur, took charge as Secretary (Food & Civil Supplies) with effect from 3-4-1998. Shri J.A. Chowdhury, relinquished charge as Secretary of Department of Sugar and Edible Oils on 19-8-1998 and Shri R.P. Sinha took over from him as Secretary, Department of Sugar & Edible Oils with effect from 19-8-1998.

Functions

The main functions of the Department of Food and Civil Supplies and Department of Sugar and Edible oils in the Ministry of Food and Consumer Affairs are:-

Department of food and civil supplies

(i) formulation and implementation of national policies on procurement, import - export, movement, public distribution and stocking of foodgrains.

(ii) provision of storage facilities for the maintenance of Central Reserves of foodgrains and promotion of Scientific storage:

(iii) entering into treaties and agreements with foreign countries in regard to trade and commerce in foodgrains and certain foodstuffs.

In carrying out its various functions, the Department of Food & Civil Supplies are assisted by their Subordinate Offices, namely the Save Grain Campaign Offices, Indian Grain Management Research Institute and its 5 Field Stations, two Public Sector Undertakings viz., the Food Corporation of India (FCI) and the Central Warehousing Corporation (CWC).

Department of sugar and edible oils

(i) fixation of statutory minimum prices of Sugarcane payable by sugar factories, development and regulations of Sugar Industry (including training of Sugar Technology), fixation of price of levy sugar and its supply for PDS and regulation of supply of free sale sugar

(ii) industries the control of which by the Union is declared by Parliament by law to be expedient in public interest, as far as these relate to Vanaspati, Oilseeds, Vegetable Oils, Cakes and Fat

(iii) price control of and inter-state trade and commerce in and supply and distribution of Vanaspati, Oilseeds, Vegetable Oils, Cakes and Fats.

In carrying out its various functions, the Department of Sugar & Edible Oils are assisted by their attached and Subordinate Offices, namely the Directorate of Sugar and Directorate of Vanaspati Vegetable Oils and Fats and National Sugar Institute, Kanpur, National Institute of Sugarcane and Sugar Technology, Mau and one Public Sector Undertaking viz., the Hindustan Vegetable Oils Corporation.

The total strength of both the Departments, including

its attached and subordinate offices as on 30.11.98 was 2162 comprising 237 posts in Group A, 398 in Group B, 876 in Group C and 651 in Group D. The details are given in Appendix-I.

O&M activities

Besides the routine O&M work like inspection of Sections/Desks, monitoring of the progress of cases pending over one months/six months compilation/consolidation of orders/instructions, etc. one special drive on records management which included recording, indexing, reviewing & weeding out of files was conducted during the year 1998-99 in both the Departments as well as its attached and subordinate offices.

As a result of the special drive, the record management was streamlined and better organised. In addition, a revised brochure on record retention schedule for uncommon records in the Departments has been brought out in consultation with the National Archives of India.

The Annual Action Plan to implement Point No. 20 (Responsive Administration) of the Twenty Point Programme, 1986 for the year 1998-99 was drawn up and the progress made in the matter was reviewed at regular intervals.

Organisation Charts of the Departments of Food and Civil Supplies and Sugar and Edible Oils are at Appendices.

Outstanding audit inspection reports

40 Audit Inspection Reports with 121 Paras were outstanding as on 30th November 1998 as against 33 Audit Inspection Reports with 99- Paragraphs outstanding as on 31st December, 1997. All efforts are being made for settling the outstanding Audit Inspection Reports/Paragraphs.

Redressal of public grievances and staff grievances

There are three Departments in the Ministry of Food & Consumer Affairs i.e. Department of Food and Civil Supplies, Department of Sugar and Edible Oils and Department of Consumer Affairs. All these Departments have a separate Director (PG) who are of the rank of Joint Secretary.

They are vested with the powers to call for the files/ papers from various Divisions of the Ministry and its attached/subordinate offices relating to grievances pending for more than three months and to take decision thereon with the approval of the Secretary of the concerned Department.

For the convenience/information of the general public the names of the Directors (PG) have 9 been incorporated in the Delhi Telephone Directory as well as internal Telephone Directory. Grievance boxes have also been placed at the easily accessible places near the entrance of the Ministry at Krishi Bhavan for receiving grievances/ complaints from members of the public. In addition, the Information and Facilitation Centres, have been set up in the Ministry.

There are two Public Sector Undertakings (PSUs) under the administrative control of the Department of Food and Civil Supplies i.e. the Food Corporation of India (FCI) and the Central Warehousing Corporation (CWC). Both these PSUs have Grievance Redressal Machinery. Executive Director in the Food Corporation of India (FCI) and an officer of the rank of Personnel Manager in the Central Warehousing Corporation (CWC) have been designated as Director of Public Grievances for redressal of Public complaints/grievances.

They have been vested with the powers to call for the files/papers from the concerned Divisions of the organizations pending for more than three months and to take decision thereon with the approval of the Managing Director of the respective PSU. Weekly meetingless day is being observed by these organizations for redressal of public grievances. Notice Boards have also been displayed by these organizations for convenience of the complainants.

Information and Facilitation Counters for the Ministry of Food and Consumer Affairs have been set up at Krishi Bhavan (Gate No. 6) with the objective of providing information to people. The Counter provides information through printed materials and computer printouts on food and civil supplies, imports of foodgrains and sugar, price and subsidy, storage.

A quarterly report of the Public Grievances received and disposed of is sent to the Department of Administrative Reforms and Public Grievances. In addition an on-line monthly return is also sent through NIC to the Department of AR&PG.

The Staff Grievances mainly relate to the delay in pay fixation, promotion, confirmation, clearing of efficiency bar etc., and providing basic amenities and work environment. Instructions have been issued by Government detailing the time period for each such activity.

Adequate transparency now exists in respect of administrative matters and the staff are free to meet on every Wednesday Director (Admn.) who has been designated as Staff Grievances Officer. Besides, Secretary (F&CS) is also available to meet the staff on Ist Wednesday of the month. There is also an Office Council and regular meetings are held under the Chairmanship of Joint Secretary (Admn.)

The position of Public and Staff Grievances for the period from 1st January 1998 to 31st December 1998 is given to the next page.

		Department	*FCI*	*CWC*
1.	No. of complaints brought forward as pending on 1.1.98	4	117	4
2.	No. of complaints received from 1.1.98 to 31.12.98	75	92	2
3.	Total No. of complaints (1+2)	79	209	6
4.	Complaints disposed of	74	111	5
5.	Balance of complaints as on 31.12.98	5	98	1

Welfare activities

In pursuance of the decision of the Committee of the Cabinet, a wholetime Welfare Officer is functioning in the Ministry with a view to maintain good employees-employer relationship. A First Aid Post is in operation in the Welfare Section. Over 500 employees of the Ministry were benefited by obtaining medical assistance for minor ailments.

Welfare Section of this Ministry organised (i) Anti-Terrorism Day and (ii) Sadbhavana Diwas during this period.

A full-fledged cricket team comprising of 16 members is participating in Inter-Ministry Cricket Tournament organised by Central Civil Services Cultural & Sports Board.

Computerisation

National Informatics Centre (NIC) being computer consultancy and promotional organisation the Government of India, has been working in close co-ordination with Ministry of Food and Consumer Affairs, since 1986. It has established Computer Centres in Krishi Bhavan and Shastri Bhavan computerise various areas of Food Management and office automation. The five year IT plan for Food sector has been prepared and submitted to the Government of India to support the availability information at different levels. The division is making all efforts to upgrade hardware and software and necessary trainings are being imparted.

To develop client-server applications for the ministry, Windows NT server has been installed on HP Netserver, and around 40 client computers are connected to it over Local Area Network (LAN). This in addition to Pentium Pro based server for database; file services and another Pentium system for mail and Internet access.

To provide fast and Graphical User Interface (GUI) based Internet access, NIC has set up a WAN using Radio Frequency Link, and Leased Lines. These three links provide redundancy and ensures connection to the Internet round the clock.

Some of the new divisions are also provided terminals to use the application developed for them a also carry out their routine jobs.

One server has been made operational and available round the clock to call data from states a districts for NICNET based applications such as Price Monitoring System, Movement Information System, Information on procurement of foodgrains and Stocks position etc.

Various Application Software have been developed and implemented in the UNIX server installed Krishi Bhavan:

An information system has been developed to monitor demand, allocation and offtake of rice and wheat under PDS

To manage library activities effectively, a package have

been developed. This system has got features like issue and return of books, acquisition of new books, maintaining of purchase orders, generating defaulters list, calculation of fine, issuing reminders etc.

To comply with the guidelines from AR&PG, every month a statement relating to status of put grievances is sent through NICNET. Necessary support is extended to the facilitation counter for department.

Price Monitoring System (PMS) has been developed and implemented at the district level and the data is sent daily/weekly to-a server to data processing and report generation.

Public Distribution system (PDS) involves issue of essential commodities to a large number of people through a network of FPS on a recurring basis. Necessary software is implemented to monitor allocation, lifting of the commodities.

Storage Information System is developed to monitor the storage capacities available and their utilization. The system provides data of various agencies namely FCI, CWC and SWC.

Stock Position: Commodity wise status of stocks available at FCI godown is being monitored on fortnightly basis. It is proposed to call data through NICNET.

Directorate of sugar

The information system for Directorate of Sugar has been developed and implemented. This includes sugar production on weekly basis from all the 474 sugar factories, monitoring of cane price arrears, allocation and monitoring of levy and free sugar, free sale realization. A system to monitor the lapses out of free sugar has been developed.

To bring transparency to the government work, the

release orders are generated with more information and circulated to the sugar industries on monthly basis.

Directorate of vanaspati

Server with UNIX operating system and with 5 terminals has been installed in Directorate of Vanaspati, Vegetable Oils and Fats. Vegetable Oils Information system has been developed and implemented. This software provides various data entry forms for all returns (Form A, B and C) for entering data of around 180 units and generating required reports.

Food corporation of India

NIC has been providing computerization services to FCI in terms of procurement of hardware, development of software, training and computer communication support.

FCI has procured FTDMA V-SAT connectivity to enhance its communication capability, and data can be transferred directly to FCI headquarters. NIC is providing technical support for establishing computer centres at around 92 FCI district offices and also providing e-mail connectivity through dial-up link at these locations. Movement Information System (MOVIS) has been implemented to monitor the movement of foodgrains all over the country.

NIC has developed "District Accounting System" for FCI and implemented in all districts in Andhra Pradesh. It is proposed to implement the software in all FCI offices.

A "Procurement Package" for FCI is developed to maintain database relating to the procurement status of rice, wheat and paddy on daily basis. The communication of data can be through NICNET. NIC has organized number of training programmes for FCI officers in the respective State units of NIC as well as at NIC headquarters.

Central warehousing corporation

Two Pentium based systems have been installed at CWC headquarters and has been equip with FTDMA V-SAT connectivity for communication.

NIC has developed softwares for the following applications, concerned division persons are being trained to make use of these softwares.

- Personnel Information System
- Business Information System
- Planning Support System
- Purchase Support System
- SWC Monitoring System
- Training Information System
- FESS -Monitoring System
- DESS, Monitoring System
- Leave Accounting System
- Loss and Gain Monitoring System

In addition to the above softwares on "Construction Cost and Estimation for a Warehouse" is under development. E-mail connection through dial-up have been established at Regional offices of CWC.

The Department is entrusted with the following work:-

i) Internal Trade.

ii) Inter State Trade: The Spirituous Preparations (Inter- State Trade and Commerce) Control Act, 1955 (39 of 1955).

iii) Control of Futures Trading: the Forward Contracts (Regulation) Act, 1952 (74 of 1952)

iv) Essential Commodities Act, 1955 (10 of 1955)

(Supply, Prices and Distribution of Essential Commodities not dealt with specifically by any other Ministry/Department).

v) Prevention of Blackmarketing and Maintenance of Supply of Essential Commodities Act, 1980 (7 of 1980). Persons subjected to detention thereunder.

vi) Regulation of Packaged Commodities.

vii) Training in Legal Metrology.

viii) Emblems and Names (Prevention of Improper Use) Act, 1952 (12 of 1952).

ix) Standards of Weights and Measures. The Standards of Weights and Measures Act, 1976 (60 of 1976).

x) Bureau of Indian Standards Act, 1986 (63 of 1986).

xi) Consumer Cooperatives.

xii) All attached or subordinate offices or other organisations concerned with any of the subject specified in this list including Forward Markets Commission, Mumbai.

xiii) Monitoring of Prices and Availability of essential commodities.

xiv) Consumer Protection Act, 1986 (68 of 1996).

Plan schemes

Agricultural development is crucial to India's overall progress and this can be achieved by intensifying the agricultural and allied activities as well as by diversification and commercialization of agriculture. A strong and effective food processing sector plays a significant role in diversification of agricultural activities, improving value addition of agricultural produce, increasing employment opportunities and creating surplus for export of agro-food products. This would, however, require policies and plans for improvement of food processing infrastructure including upgradation of technology and enforcement of quality standards, activating domestic market with focus on exports. Taking this into account, the 9th Five Year Plan has been formulated with special emphasis on the following:

i. Creation of infrastructure including cold chain infrastructure

ii. Quality Upgradation and quality control

iii. Research & development

iv. Special incentives for the North-Eastern States, Jammu and Kashmir, hilly areas, backward areas' including tribal areas.

The Ministry of Food Processing Industries has been operating several plan schemes for the development of processed food industry since the inception of 8th plan period. Taking into account the recommendations of the Working Group of Planning Commission, the constraints faced by the industry, the need to accelerate growth of the sector and the priority status accorded to food processing industry by Government, the Ministry of Food Processing Industries is operating the following plan schemes during the 9th Plan:

Scheme for development of infrastructural facilities

The main objectives of the scheme is to:

i) Establish post-harvest infrastructure and cold chain facilities for food processing as well as integrated projects of mushroomshops, gherkins and baby corn.

ii) Establish food processing industrial estates/food parks.

iii) Createinfrastructural facilities for preservation and processing of fish.

Scheme for setting tip/expansion/modernization of food processing industries

The main objective of the scheme is

i) Setting up/expansion/modernization of food processing units.

ii) Modernization of pulse milling units—The objective of this scheme is installation of dryers and dust control systems for drying of pulses & control of dust during processing for increasing productivity and efficiency.

iii) Setting up of mobile fruit & vegetable processing units - The objective of this scheme is propagation of the concept of mobile fruit and vegetable processing facilities which takes the facility of processing to the doorsteps of the farmers.

iv) Dissemination of low cost preservation technology - The objective of this scheme is to -encourage setting up units using low cost preservation technology.

Scheme for development/modernization of meat processing

The objective of the scheme is development of meat processing industries to achieve good quality, hygienic production of meat and meat products, and development/propagation of international quality standards through modernization of abattoirs, adoption of HACCPA & ISO standards, and evolving an effective quality assurance system.

Scheme for development of poultry & egg processing

The objective of the scheme is development of processed poultry and egg products for both domestic and export markets, with assured quality and health standards and also for effecting necessary technological improvement of processing units.

Scheme for research and development

1. Undertake specific R&D Projects on/relating to:
    - i. Processing of cereals, pulses, coarse grains and millets and also for improving traditional/regional foods made from them.
    - ii. Study of prevailing post-harvest technology of millets like ragi, jowar and bajra and devise improvements thereto.
    - iii. Development of processing technology for the production of intermediate and finished food products including design and building -of prototype equipment/pilot plants.
    - iv. Fortification of cereals/cereal products for enhancing the nutritional level of our population, especially women and children.
    - V. Traditional foods of various regions of the country; and
    - vi. Utilization of by-products of primary food processing like paddy husk, germ, paddy-straw, pulse-corn, peri carp brokens etc.
2. Update processing, packing and storage technologies for all major processed food products so that they meet international standards.
3. Standardization of various factors such as bacteriological standards, level of preservatives, additives, pesticide residue etc. of meat and meat products, development of value added products of commercial importance.
4. Take Lip research & development work for traditional milk products and packaging of milk products.

5. Development of value added products Using low value fish, product development, standardization of processing technology for non-conventional marine resources like snails, clams, mussels, oysters, etc.

6. Development of new cost effective packaging for food products based oil traditional foods, common food grains, dairy products etc., for both domestic and export purposes. Development of design of equipment for manufacture of such products, development of new inexpensive packaging techniques and equipments, analysis of existing packaging methods, material processes, quality control norms studies about improvement in the currently used systems, Studies about newer packaging possibilities.

7. Financial assistance Would also be available for Setting Lip of quality control laboratory for all processed foods.

Scheme for personpower development

The scheme has the following six components:-

i) Personpower development in rural areas (Food Processing & Training Centres).

   The objectives of this scheme is development of rural entrepreneurship and transfer of technology for processing of food products by ctilising locally grown raw materials and providing 'hands oil' experience at such product ion-cum-training centres, while according priority to persons belonging to SCs/STs/OBCs and women.

ii) Personpower development in grain processing industries of raw materials/finished products, preventive maintenance, sailitation, hygiene and development of organizational and planning abilities.

iii) Training of personpower in meat processing.

The objective of the scheme is training of persons engaged in traditional meat processing activity, in-service workers and unemployed persons.

iv) Training of traditional fisherpersons for skill upgradation in fish processing.

The objectives of the scheme is training of persons engaged in fish processing units for upgrading the quality of products and improving hygienic conditions.

v) Creation of Infrastructural facilities.

The objective of this scheme is to create infrastructual facilities like library, laboratories, pilot plants etc. for running Degree/diploma Courses and training programmes for food processing.

vi) Training programmes sponsored by MFPI.

The objective of the scheme is to conduct training programmes sponsored by Ministry of food processing in various areas of food processing.

Scheme for strengthening of traditional fish processing technologies and marketing

This scheme aims at propagation of low cost indigenous technologies for drying of fish, which will result in value addition, and provide hygienically dried fish for domestic and export market.

Scheme for utilization of low value fish to make value added products

The objective of this scheme is establishment of units for commercial production of value added products like protein concentrates, fish wafers, fish sausages, fish soup, fish cutlets, fish balls, fish feed etc., using low value fish.

Scheme for setting up of innovative dairy projects

The objective of the scheme is to encourage introduction of innovative dairy items such as whey protein, protein concentrates, extraction of minerals, casein etc., where new technology and higher value addition is involved.

Scheme for development/improvement of marketing, quality control, storage & transport of meat & meat products

The objective of the scheme is to provide deep freezers/ refrigerators to retail outlets, marketing complexes for development of meat markets and shopping centres, provision Of insulators, refrigerated/children vans for transportation of meat, and establishment/improvement of quality control laboratories.

Scheme for generic advertisement on processed foods and marketing assistance

The objective of the scheme is to build awareness among consumers about the advantages of processed foods, and their quality assurance mechanism, both through (i) Generic Advertisement and Publicity and (ii) Market Promotion Campaign for new product mix and brand name support.

Scheme for strengthening of backward linkages in food processing industries

The objective of the scheme is to

i) Increase capacity utilization of fruit & vegetable processing units as well as grain and coarse grain, processing units by ensuring regular supply of raw materials through contract farming;

ii) Ensure remunerative price to farmers by creating direct linkage between farmers and processors; and

iii) Provide high quality seeds/ fertilizers/ pesticides and planting materials to farmers along with technical know-how etc., through the processor.

Scheme for promotion of food processing industries

The objective of the scheme is to :

i) Strengthen the Directorate of Fruit & vegetable Preservation for information, education and quality systems.

ii) Participation in national/international exhibitions/ fairs.

iii) Promotion of studies, surveys etc., in the food processing sector.

iv) Performance awards.

Scheme for strengthening of nodal agencies

The objective of the scheme is to strengthen the designated State Nodal Agencies for food processing by providing financial support for installation of basic office hardware including computer system and internet for collection of detailed field information, preparation of data base, monitoring of assisted projects, coordination of agro food business etc.

Nature of assistance

The assistance under various plan schemes is available to PSUs/Joint Sector/Assisted Sector/NGOs/ Cooperatives and to private entrepreneurs in the form of grant-in-aid and soft loan. However, a higher level of assistance is provided to NGOs/Cooperatives. Special incentives are provided for projects in "difficult areas" like North-Eastern States, Jammu& Kashmir, and Sikkim, island areas and tribal areas.

Special component plan & tribal sub-plan

The Schemes formulated by the Ministry are aimed at providing facilities and incentives for promotion of food processing industries in the country. These schemes envisage enhanced scale of assistance for "difficult" areas, including Integrated Tribal Development Project (ITDP) areas. The Schemes from which benefit of plan assistance may accrue to tribal areas and to SC/ST Communities, are indicated below:

Scheme for development of infrastructural facilities

This scheme -envisages financial assistance In the form of grant to PSUs/joint sector/NGOs and cooperatives to the extent of 50% of the cost of capital equipment and technical civil works up to Rs. 25 lakhs in general areas whereas in the case of difficult areas, assistance will be 75% Lip to Rs.50 lakhs. However, loans to PSUs and joint sector units Would be 50% of the total equity subject to a maximum of Rs. 150 lakhs in general areas and Rs.200 lakhs in difficult areas.

Scheme for setting up/expansion/modernisation of food processing industries

Under this scheme, PSUs are eligible to get loan up to 50% of cost of capital equipment and technical civil works up to Rs.150 lakhs in general areas and Rs.200 lakhs in difficult areas or grant Up to 50% of cost of capital equipment and technical civil works up to Rs.50 lakhs in difficult areas would be available. Alternatively, such joint sector units call get grant up to 25% cost of capital cost of technical civil works up to Rs.25 lakhs in difficult areas. In the case of private/assisted sector, loan Up to 50% and up to Rs.50 lakhs in general areas would be provided whereas in the case of difficult areas, they Would be given up to Rs. 75 lakhs. For NGOs and cooperatives, financial assistance in the form of grant up to Rs.25 lakhs in general areas and 50% up to Rs.50 lakhs in difficult areas is provided.

Scheme for development/modernization of meat processing industries

Under this scheme, NGOs, cooperatives, civic bodies and

Government organizations are eligible to get grant up to 50% of cost of capital equipment and technical civil works up to Rs.150 lakhs in general areas and 75% of such Cost up to Rs.100 lakhs in difficult areas. In the case of PSUs and joint sector units, assistance will be in the form of grant of up to 75% of cost of capital equipment and technical civil works up to Rs. 100 lakhs in difficult areas. However, assistance in the form of loan would be limited to 50% of cost of capital equipment and technical civil works up to Rs.150 lakhs in general areas and up to Rs.200 lakhs in difficult areas. In the case of private/ assisted sector, assistance will be in the form of grant Up to 50% cost of capital equipment and technical civil works up to Rs. 50 lakhs in difficult areas. For difficult areas, it will be up to Rs.75 lakhs.

Scheme for development of poultry & egg processing

This scheme envisages financial assistance to NGOs and cooperatives in the form of grant up to 50% of the cost of capital equipment and technical civil works up to Rs.75 lakhs in general areas and 75% of such cost up to Rs. 100 lakhs in difficult areas. PSUs and joint sector units are entitled to grant up to 75% of cost of capital equipment and technical civil works up to Rs. 100 lakhs in difficult areas. Assistance in the form of loan Would however be limited to 50% of cost of capital equipments and technical civil works up to Rs.150 lakhs in general areas and up to Rs.200 lakhs in difficult areas. Private and assisted sector units would be eligible to get loan up to 50% of the cost of capital equipments and technical civil works up to Rs.50 lakhs for general areas however in difficult areas, it will be up to, Rs.75 lakhs.

Scheme for strengthening of traditional fish processing and marketing

This scheme envisages financial assistance in the form of

grant to NGOs/Cooperatives/joint/assisted/private sector/PSUs up to 50% of the capital Cost up to Rs.10 lakhs in general areas and 75% of the capital cost up to Rs.10 lakhs in difficult areas.

Scheme for Utilisation of Low Value Fish

This scheme envisages financial assistance in the form of grant to NGOs/Cooperatives Up to 50% of the capital cost up to Rs. 10 lakhs in general areas and 75% of the capital cost up to Rs. 10 lakhs in difficult areas.

Though the main Concept Of Our scheme is based Oil project approach, yet about 20% of our plan funds may get apportioned to the schemes benefiting SC/ST Communities.

Promotion of food processing industries

The Ministry provides assistance for setting up, expansion and modernisation of food processing units including modernisation of pulse milling units.

Fruit & vegetable processing

During the period under review the Ministry provided loan of Rs.20 lakhs to M/s. Aaren Food Private Ltd., Bhubaneshwar for setting up of a unit at Kantabada In Kliurda District in the State of Orissa for manufacture of processed fruits and vegetables.

The Ministry provided financial assistance of Rs.8.51 lakhs to People Action For Rural Development Association (PARDA) for setting up of fruit & vegetable processing unit at Kachi Village in Ukhrul District of Manipur. The Ministry provided a grant of Rs.] 1.2 lakh to Malom Tuliyaima Development Association, Manipur for setting up of a fruit and vegetable processing unit in Bishnupur District.

An assistance of Rs. 10.7 lakh was provided to Rural

Areas Development Association, (RADA), Manipur for setting up of bamboo shoot processing plant at New Lukhambi in Tamenglong district.

Pork processing

Ministry approved an assistance of Rs.298 lakhs to State Federation of Piggery Farmers, Nagaland for establishment of Integrated Pork Processing Project in Medzifema, Dimapur. Out of this assistance of Rs. 99 lakhs was provided during the period under review. The unit is under construction.

The Assam Livestock and Poultry Corporation was also approved a grant of Rs. 175 lakhs for establishment of an Integrated Pork Processing Project at Nazira. The project is in the final stages of implementation.

In the state of Orissa, a project on Integrated Pork Processing was sanctioned and grant-in-aid of Rs.100 lakhs has been approved. Out of this, an assistance of Rs.33 lakhs has been provided during the period under review.

The Ministry has approved a grant-in-aid of Rs. 65 lakhs to MAFCO, Koregaon, Maharashtra for modernisation of meat processing plant. Out of this amount, Rs.32.5 lakhs has been released during the Current year.

Cereal based products

An amount of Rs. 25 Lakhs has been provided to Messrs. North Lakhimpur Food Processors Pvt. Ltd. Co., North Lakhimpur, Assam as grant for setting up of a biscuit manufacturing unit.

Development of infrastructure facility

Development of food processing infrastructure is essential for growth of a strong food processing sector.

The Ministry provides financial assistance for establishment of post-harvest infrastructure and cold chain facilities and food processing and for integrated projects of mushrooms, hops, gherkins, etc., setting up of food processing industrial estates and food parks; and infrastructure facilities for preservation and processing of fish. Establishment and strengthening of post harvest infrastructure helps in reducing wastage of agriculture raw material and ensures availability of agro products throughout the year for the processing unit as well as for direct consumption.

During the year under review Ministry provided a grant of Rs.14.97 lakhs to M/s. Vandaninadu Development Society, Kerala (Non- Government Organisation) for setting up of a spawn lab at Idukki in the State of Kerala.

During the year M/s. Khamderaya Grape Growers Cooperative Society have been provided a grant of Rs. 15.22 lakhs for setting LIP of a cold storage at Sangli in the State of Maharashtra.

M/s. Khyati Cold Storage Limited have been provided a loan of Rs.25 lakhs during the year for setting up of a cold storage in the State of Gujarat.

5

Food Management

The main ingredients of the Government's food management policy are procurement of foodgrains; their storage, movement, public distribution; and the maintenance of buffer stocks. These and other related aspects of this policy, such as production, procurement and issue prices of foodgrains, quality control, imports and exports, behaviour of market prices, etc. during the year 1997-98 are discussed in the succeeding paragraphs.

Annual review of foodgrains

Rainfall situation

During the monsoon season of 1998 (June to September), 33 out of 35 meteorological subdivisions and 81 % of districts of the country received normal to excess rainfall. For the country as a whole, the total rainfall during the monsoon season was 106% of its long period average value, with satisfactory spatial and temporal distribution situation. The year 1998 has been the eleventh consecutive normal monsoon year.

At the end of monsoon season, cumulative seasonal rainfall was excess in 13 and normal in 20 meteorological sub-divisions, covering 89% area of the country The rainfall was marginally deficient in only two sub-divisions viz. Orissa (-25%) and East Madhya Pradesh (-25%). During 1998, 81 % of the districts received normal to excess rainfall.

A severe cyclonic storm formed in the Arabian sea in

the month of June, 1998 caused heavy loss of life and property in Gujarat and heavy rains in West Rajasthan.

Foodgrains production performance during 1997-98

During 1997-98, the production of Rice was 82.30 million tonnes as against the production of 81.73 million tonnes during 1996-97. The production of wheat was 65.90 million tonnes during 1997-98 as against the production level of 69.35 million tonnes during 1996-97.

The production of coarse cereals during 1997-98 is estimated at 31.16 million tonnes as against the production level of 34.11 million tonnes during 1996-97.

The overall production of foodgrains during 1997-98 was estimated at 192.43 million tonnes as against the production level of 199.44 million tonnes achieved during 1996-97.

Crop outlook for 1998-99

The Planning Commission has set the targets of foodgrains production for 1998-99 at 204.00 million tonnes. The broad crop wise break up of production during 1997-98 vis-a-vis the targets set by Planning Commission for 1998-99 are as under:

Cropwise targets and advance estimates of production for 1998-99

Million tonnes

Crop	*Target 1997-98*	*Production 1997-98*	*Target 1998-99*	*Advance Estimates 98-99*
			(Provisional)	
Rice	83.00	82.30	84.40	82.23
Wheat	68.50	65.90	70.30	69.13
Coarse Cereals	33.50	31.16	33.80	29.11
Pulses	15.00	13.07	15.50	14.78
Total Foodgrains	200.00	192.43	204.00	195.25

Price position of foodgrains

The wholesale price index number of Rice moved up from 366.00 in April, 1998 to 409.9 in Dec., 1998 indicating a rise of 12.0 percent. The WPI of Wheat also rose from 334.4 to 377.5 representing a rise of 12.9 percent during the period under reference.

The WPI of Cereals increased by 12.1 percent from 348.3 in April, 1998 to 390.6 in Dec., 1998. Similarly, the WPI of foodgrains firmed up from 361.3 to 409.8 registering a rise of 13.4 percent.

Procurement

In keeping with the national policy of providing price support to the major foodgrains of the country viz., wheat, paddy and coarsegrains, the Government continued to procure foodgrains conforming to prescribed specifications offered by the farmers at the notified Minimum Support Prices (MSP).

The price support operations for wheat and paddy were undertaken by the Food Corporation of India in association with the State agencies. Paddy/Rice has been reclassified into two categories viz.

Common and Grade'A' varieties for MSP purposes for 1998-99 Kharif Marketing Season. The MSP for Common and Grade'A' variety of paddy has been fixed at Rs. 440/- and Rs. 470/- per quintal respectively for the current 1998-99 Kharif Marketing Season (October-September).

A Central bonus of Rs. 55/- per quintal has been allowed over and above MSP of wheat payable to the farmers for wheat sold to public procuring agencies during the period from 1.4.98 to 30.6.98. The comparative MSP of wheat & paddy for the 1997-98 and 1998-99 seasons are given to the next page.

(Price in Rs. per quintal)

Wheat		Paddy Common	Grade'A'
1997-98	415.00 + 60.00 (Central	415.00	445.00
1998-89.	455.00 + 55.00 bonus)	440.00	470.00

Besides extending price support to farmers for wheat and paddy, rice was also procured under levy from rice millers/dealers at the prices announced separately for each State.

Rice

The procurement of rice for the Central Pool (including paddy in terms of rice) during 1997-98 Kharif Marketing Season (October 1997-September 1998) was 14.31 million tonnes as against 12.22 million tonnes during the previous season. A quantity of 5.49 million tonnes of rice was- procured as on 22.12.98 for Central Pool during the current 1998-99 Marketing Season, as against 7.08 million tonnes procured during the corresponding period last year. Procurement of rice is in progress and is likely to be in the range of 11 to 12 million tonnes.

Wheat

The wheat procurement during 1997-98 Rabi Marketing Season was 9.30 million tonnes as against 8.16 million tonnes during 1996-97 season. In the 1998-99 Rabi Marketing Season 12.65 million tonnes of wheat was procured for Central Pool. The State-wise procurement of wheat is given in the following Table:-

(in lakh tonnes)

S.No.	State/UT	1996-97	1997-98	1998-99 upto (22.12.98)
1	Bihar	—	Neg.	Neg.

2.	Gujarat	-	-	0.02
3.	Haryana	20.21	22.90	31.58
4.	Himachal Pradesh	-	-	Neg.
5.	Jammu & Kashmir	-	-	-
6.	Madhya Pradesh	0.04,	10.07	5.31
7.	Punjab	56.42	59.61	61.45
8.	Rajasthan	2.29	3.20	6.67
9.	Uttar Pradesh	2.61	6.18	21.41
10.	Chandigarh	-	0.02	-
11.	Delhi		Neg.	0.08
	All India Total:	81.57	101.98	126.53

Neg: Below 500 Tonnes.

From the 1990-91 Rabi Marketing Season, FCI became the nodal agency for the procurement of Rabi and Kharif Coarsegrains throughout the country. The Minimum Support Price of coarse grains viz. Jowar, Bajra, Ragi and Maize was fixed at Rs. 390/- per quintal and for Barley at Rs. 350/- per quintal for 1998-99 Kharif/Rabi marketing Season over the procurement price of Rs. 360/- per quintal for Jowar, Bajra, Ragi and Maize and Rs 305/- per quintal for Barley in 1997-98 Kharif/Rabi Marketing Season. However, as the prevailing open market prices of coarsegrains were generally much higher than the Minimum Support Price, the procurement of coarsegrains has been negligible.

It has been the policy of Government of India to treat the entire country as a single food zone. Free movement of wheat, wheat products, coarsegrains and levy-free rice is permissible throughout the country.

Central issue price

Wheat and rice are issued from the Central Pool to State Govts./UTs at uniform Central Issue Prices for distribution under TPDS. The CIP of foodgrains issued under the TPDS are fixed below the economic cost and Central Government bears a huge subsidy burden on this account.

Consequent upon the decision of the Central Government to streamline and restructure PDS with focus on the poor (the Targeted PDS), the CIP (Ex-FCI godowns) of wheat and rice issued from Central Pool have since been revised from 1st June, 1997. Movement of wheat, non-levy rice remained free throughout the country. However, some State Governments like J&K, West Bengal & A.P have imposed certain restrictions on the movement of paddy/rice. They are being persuaded to remove these restrictions.

Procurement of rice

Marketing Season:

(October-September)

(in lakh tonnes)

S.No.	*State/U/T.*	*1996-97*	*1997-98*	*1998-99*
1	Andhra Pradesh	45.25	38.42	7.25
2.	Assam	0.01	-	-
3.	Bihar	Neg.	0.21	-
4.	Haryana	12.05	12.65	1.83
5.	Karanataka	0.83	0.91	0.29
6.	Madhya Pradesh	5.80	10.27	0.79
7.	Maharashtra	0.32	0.26	Neg.
8.	Orissa	4.77	7.00	0.88
9.	Punjab	42.31	60.36	40.84
10.	Rajasthan	0.03	0.06	0.02
11.	Tamil Nadu	7.37	12.50	0.30
12.	Uttar Pradesh	9.11	10.73	2.94
13.	West Bengal	1.59	2.02	-
14.	Chandigarh	0.14	0.11	0.05
15.	Pondicherry	0.05	0.08	0.01
16.	Delhi	-	-	Neg.
Total		129.63	155.58	55.20

Procurement operations in tribal and non-traditional areas

The TRIFED under the Ministry of Welfare procures

foodgrains in tribal areas on behalf of FCI under price support, and foodgrains so procured by TRIFED are handed over to FCI. Proposal is also under consideration of the Government to decentralise the procurement of foodgrains by encouraging the State Governments/ Agencies to procure and distribute rice/wheat within the State and claim subsidy from the Central Government.

Levy

There is no levy on basmati rice, wheat, coarsegrains and pulses. Government undertakes to purchase all wheat and paddy of prescribed specifications offered for sale by the farmers, thereby ensuring them of a stable market for their produce. Non-basmati rice is procured for the Central Pool under statutory levy system imposed by the State Governments in exercise of powers conferred on them under the Essential Commodities Act, 1955. The percentage of levy varies from State to State as may be seen from the statement at next page.

Taking into account the availability of rice in the Central Pool, the increasing demand for TPDS and other welfare schemes, Government of India has not agreed to granting exemption to any variety of non-basmati rice, either for internal market or for export, from levy obligation in Kharif Marketing Season 1997-98. The States/UTs have been requested to implement the Levy Orders strictly. During the 199899 Kharif Season, due to damage caused to paddy by unseasonal rains exemption from levy was granted to Punjab upto 10. 10.98, and in Haryana upto 31.10.98. In the context of the rising prices of wheat in the open market, in December, 1996, with a view to curb hoarding and black-marketing of wheat and wheat-products, all the States/UTs. were advised to reimpose licensing/stock limits on wheat and wheat products. Most of the States/UTs have taken action in this regard. Punjab has not favoured keeping stock-limits.

System of procurement of rice during 1998-99 Kharif marketing season

S.No.	*Name of the State/UT*	*Category*	*Quantum of Levy*
1.	Andhra Pradesh	Millers/Dealers	50%
2.	Assam	Millers/Dealers	50%
3.	Bihar	No levy from April, 1989	-
4.	Gujarat	Millers	2%*
5.	Haryana	Millers/Dealers	75%
6.	Karnataka	Millers/Dealers	331/3%
7.	Madhya Pradesh	Millers/Dealers	50%
8.	Maharashtra	Millers	30%
9.	Orissa	Millers	75%
10.	Punjab	Millers/Dealers	75%
11.	Rajasthan	Millers/Dealers	25%
12.	Tamil Nadu	Millers/Dealers	50%
13.	Uttar Pradesh	Millers/Dealers	60%
			40%
14.	West Bengal	Millers	30%
15.	Chandigarh	Millers/Dealers	75%
16.	Delhi	Millers/Dealers	75%
17.	Pondicherry	Millers/Dealers	10%

Buffer stocking policy

The importance of building up a buffer stock of foodgrains to stabilise the food economy of the country has tong been recognised. In fact, adequate size of buffer stock of foodgrains in an essential element of the national food policy. Buffer stock of foodgrains is necessary not only to impart interseasonal stability to foodgrains supply and prices, but also to ensure food security and meet emergent situations arising out of unexpected crop failures, natural disasters etc.

The Government in December, 1990, fixed the level of minimum stocks to be maintained by the public agencies on different dates of a year during the 8th Five Year Plan period as under:-

(in million tonnes)

Date	*Rice*	*Wheat*	*Total*
1 at April	10.8	3.7	14.5
1st July	9.2	13.1	22.3
1st October	6.0	10.6	16.6
1st January	7.7	7.7	15.4

The Government had constituted a Technical Group on Buffer Stocks of Foodgrains in November, 1995, under the Chairmanship of the then Secretary, Food Procurement & Buffer Stocking Policy of Foodgrains for the Ninth Plan Period. After careful consideration of the Report submitted by the Group, Government has vide Orders issued on 30th October, 1998, fixed minimum requirement of stock for the remaining period of the Ninth five year Plan as under with immediate effect:-

Prescribed minimum stock levels

(in million tonnes)

Date	*Rice*	*Wheat*	*Total*
1st April	11.8	4.0	15.8
1st July	10.0	14.3	24.3
1st October		11.6	18.1
1st January	8.4	8.4	16.8

Stock position

As on 1.10.97, the stocks of foodgrains in the Central Pool held by FCI and State Agencies stood at 15.34 million tonnes as against 19.88 million tonnes on the same day in the preceding year. The total stock of foodgrains in the

Central Pool - as on 1st October during the last five years were as follows:-

(in million tonnes)

1.10.1994	26.45 (P)
1.10.1995	29.95 (P)
1.10.1996	19.88 (P)
1.10.1997	15.34 (P)
1.10.1998	24.20 (P)

(P) = Provisional

The following table gives provisional stock position in the Central Pool vis-a-vis minimum buffer norms:-

(in million tonnes)

	Wheat		*Rice*		*Total*	
Date	*Actual stock*	*Minimum buffer norms*	*Actual stock*	*Minimum buffer norms*	*Actual stock*	*Minimum buffer norms*
1.1.1998	6.76	7.70	11.48	7.70	18.24	15.40
1.4.1998	5.07	3.70	13.05	10.80	18.12	14.50
1.7.1998	16.47	13.10	12.04	9.20	28.51	22.30
1.10.1998	15.24	10.60	8.96	6.00	24.20	16.60

Import of foodgrains

Government after reviewing the stock position of wheat and trend of production during 1997-98 (Rabi Season) decided to import upto 20 lakh tonnes of wheat during 1998-99 and authorised the STC to take steps for import of wheat. The STC finalised contracts for import of 15 lakh tonnes (*5%) of wheat from Australia. Government subsequently decided not to go in for import of the remaining quantity of 5 lakh tonnes of wheat. Against the contracted quantity of 15 lakh tonnes, 14.15 lakh tonnes of wheat has already been received. The stock position of rice in the Central Pool is comfortable and there is no need to import rice for the present or in the near future.

Government has allowed free import of common/ coarse varieties of rice and rice with 50% or more brokens. The Roller Flour Mills have also been allowed to import wheat freely under Actual User condition either directly or through STC, PEC or MMTC to meet their own requirements for milling purposes only.

Export of foodgrains

As per the current EXIM Policy export of -basmati and non-Basmati rice is allowed freely, while export of wheat, wheat products, coarsegrains and pulses is subject to export ceilings fixed from time to time. In view of the tight stock position of wheat in the country, Government had stopped issue of Registration-cum-Allocation Certificates (RCACs) for export of wheat and wheat products w.e.f. 8.1.97.

The Government of India have since released the following quantitative ceilings for export of wheat products and coarsegrains during the licensing year 1998-99.

1.	Wheat Products	1.00 lakh MTs
2.	Coarsegrains	1.00 lakh MTs

No export ceiling has been released in respect of pulses during 1998-99 but export of pulses in consumer packs upto 5.00 kg has been freely allowed.

There was no export of foodgrains (wheat and rice) from the Central Pool during the year **199899** except a quantity of 20,000 tonnes of non-basmati rice gifted to the Bangladesh Government as flood relief.

Public distribution system

'Rationing was first introduced in India in 1939 in Bombay. In 1943 the First Foodgrain Policy Committee recommended continuation of rationing due to the fall of Burma, which was a major supplier of rice, and the Great Bengal Famine in the preceding year. Immediately after Independence, rationing was abolished, only to be reintroduced in 1950, as shortages led to high prices. The rationing system introduced due to scarcity of food during this period evolved into the present day Public Distribution System (PDS) in the mid 1960s characterised by near self sufficiency in foodgrains production, holding of huge buffer stocks of foodgrains by the Government and rapid expansion of the network of distribution outlets deep into the rural areas of the country. The Public Distribution System (PDS), has, over the years, become an important instrument of Government's policy of ensuring availability of foodgrains to the public at affordable price regulating the open market prices of essential commodities and enhancing food security at the household level.

Under the PDS the Central Government has assumed responsibility for procurement and supply of essential commodities, viz. wheat, rice, levy sugar, imported edible oil and kerosene to the State Governments and the Union Territories for distribution at almost uniform and affordable prices to the public. These commodities are made available to the States/UTs at fixed Central Issue Prices (CIPs) which are determined by the Central Government and generally involve subsidies borne by the Central Government. Some States/UTs also distribute additional items of mass consumption through the PDS outlets, i.e. the Fair Price Shops (FPSs).

The implementation of PDS is the joint responsibility of the Central Government and the State Governments/UT Administrations. The Central Government is responsible for procurement, storage and transportation of the PDS commodities up to the Central godowns and making them available to the States. The responsibility for distribution to the consumers through the Fair Price Shops and administration of the PDS rests with the State Governments and UT Administration. State-wise population, number of households, number of ration cards and number of fair price shops are given in Table

Advisory Council

Advisory Council on Public Distribution has been renamed as the Advisory Council on Foodgrains Management and Public Distribution as recommended by the Sarkaria Commission. The council is an apex level body to advise the Government on all matters relating to the foodgrains management, functioning of the Public Distribution System and management of supplies of essential commodities and to suggest measures necessary for further improvement of the distribution arrangements by the public agencies.

Allocation and offtake

An Inter-Ministerial Committee on Allocation of PDS commodities under the Chairmanship of Secretary, Department of Food & Civil supplies consider and finalise allocation of PDS commodities to States/UTs every month. Secretaries in the Ministry of Petroleum and Natural Gas-and Department of Sugar & Edible Oils are members of the Committee.

State-wise allocation and lifting of rice, wheat, sugar, imported edible oils and kerosene under the Public Distribution System during 1998-99 (upto December 98) is at Table-II.

A total quantity of about 128.32 lakh tonnes of rice and 101.14 lakh tonnes of wheat was allotted to various States/ UTs for PDS (including Defence, CRPF, Bhutan etc.) during 1997-98. A quantity of 107.37 lakh tonnes of rice and 83.59 lakh tonnes of wheat has been allotted during April, 98 to January 1999 to States/UTs for distribution under TPDS, during 1998-99. This includes the quantities allotted for Defence/CRPF/BSF and Bhutan.

The position of allotment and offtake of rice and wheat under Public Distribution System, including CRPF/BSF/ Defence & Bhutan since 1991-92 is given below:-

As per the present policy, coarsegrains procured in any State/UT are allotted to the same State/UT for utilisation under Public Distribution System. During 1997-98 Kharif Marketing Season, a total quantity of 1957 tonnes of Maize in Andhra Pradesh; 3997 tonnes of Maize, 1162 tonnes of Bajra and 288 tonnes of Jowar in Madhya Pradesh; 824 tonnes of Maize and 4808 tonnes of Jowar in Maharashtra and 2809 tonnes of Maize and 4711 tonnes of Jowar in Gujarat was procured. The coarsegrains procured have been allotted to respective States for distribution under TPDS. In view of difficulties in distribution of coarsegrains in Andhra Pradesh and Madhya Pradesh, permission has been granted to FCI to dispose of unutilised stocks by tenders.

Besides PDS, foodgrains are also issued under following Schemes:

(i) Jawahar rojgar yojna/employment assurance schemes

As in the past years, a quantity, of 12,00 lakh MTs of foodgrains, 5.5 lakh MT Rice and 6.5 lakh MT wheat was placed at the disposal of M/o Rural Areas & Employment for utilisation under JRY/EAS during 1998-99 at Economic Cost. The lifting has been as under:-

(in lakh Tonnes)

Year	*Rice*	*Wheat*
1995-96	0.50	0.84
1996-97	0.42	0.65
1997-98	0.03	0.01

No offtake has been reported during 1998-99 till October 1998.

(ii)Wheat based Nutrition Programmes (NP)

Against a quantity of 1.00 lakh MT wheat allotted annually for NP, a quantity of 1.50 lakh MT wheat was placed at the disposal of M/o Social Justice and Empowerment under the scheme during 1996-97 and 1997-98. The same quantity has been allotted for 1998-99 also at Economic Cost. The quantity of wheat lifted under the scheme during 1996-97 was 1.47 lakh MT For 1997-98, a quantity of 1.5 lakh MT of wheat was allotted under this scheme at Economic Cost and a quantity of 0.53 lakh MT wheat has been lifted. During 1998-99 till October 1998, 0.13 lakh MT of wheat has been reported to have been lifted.

(iii) Supply of foodgrains at concessional rates to SC/ ST/OBC hostels

The scheme was commenced in October, 1994. The foodgrains were supplied to the States/UTs by FCI at the then RPDS rates. The actual requirement has been assessed by the erstwhile M/o Welfare at 2 45 lakh MT (wheat & rice). During 1995-96, about 2.12 lakh MT rice and 0.04 lakh MT wheat was lifted under the scheme. The lifting has been only about 1. 18 lakh MT rice and 0.05 lakh MT wheat during 1996-97. From 1997-98, foodgrains are issued by FCI at Economic Cost. An offtake of 0.23 lakh MT rice and 0.01 lakh MT wheat has been reported during 1997-98. No offtake has been reported during 1998-99 upto October 1998.

(iv) Employment generation scheme in rural areas

Commencing from October 1994, the foodgrains (rice & wheat) were to be issued to States/UTs at Rs. 1600 per MT less than the CIP for PDS for Employment Generation for manufacturing food products by BPL families in the Rural Areas & Urban Areas, for a period of five years. Out of a quantity of 5.0 lakh MTs of foodgrains (rice & wheat) earmarked per annum for this scheme, 3.5 lakh MT was meant for rural areas and 1.5 lakh MT for Urban areas. The scheme for urban areas has since been dropped.

The lifting has been as under:-

(In lakh Tonnes)

Year	*Rice*	*Wheat*
1995-96	0.08	0.08
1996-97	0.00	0.00
1997-98	0.00	0.00

From 1997-98 the foodgrains are issued at Economic Cost as per the decision of Ministry of Finance. No offtake was reported during 1997-98. No offtake has been reported during 1998-99 also upto October 1998.

(v) Mid-day meals scheme

This scheme was launched by the M/o HRD (D/o Education) during 1995-96 from 15.8.95 for the benefit of the students in the primary schools in RPDS/EAS blocks (2368). Foodgrains (rice & wheat) are supplied by FCI free of cost to the States/UTs. However, FCI charges the economic cost of the foodgrains supplied under the scheme from the M/o HRD, D/o Education. A quantity of 3.74 lakh MT rice and 1.91 lakh MT wheat was lifted under the scheme during 1995-96. The scheme had been extended to all other Low Female Literacy (LFL) blocks (2005) during 1996-97 and to all primary schools in the country (828 blocks) & 3000 odd Nagar Palikas during 1997-98, A quantity of 27.07 lakh MT of foodgrains (17.46 lakh MT rice and 9.61 lakh MT wheat) has been allotted under the scheme during 1998-99. A quantity of about 5.79 lakh MT rice and 4.01 lakh MT wheat is reported to have been lifted under this scheme during 1996-97. During 1997-98 a quantity of 12.42 lakh MT rice and 6.55

lakh MT wheat is reported to have been lifted under this scheme. A quantity of 3.69 lakh tonnes of rice and 1.08 lakh tonnes of wheat has been lifted during 1998-99 upto October 1998.

Targeted Public Distribution System (TPDS)

The importance of an effective PDS that ensures availability of food at affordable prices at household level for the poor can hardly be over emphasised. A scheme for distribution of foodgrains at specially subsidised prices in ITDP areas was introduced in December, 1985. These tribal areas became the part of the Revamped Public Distribution System (RPDS) which was launched by the Prime Minister in 1992 with the objective of improving the reach of PDS to the vulnerable sections living not only in these areas but also in other poor areas, such as drought prone, deserts and hill areas. Under RPDS foodgrains were supplied for about 1775 identified blocks to the States/Union Territories at 50 paise per kg. less than the Central Issue Price.

However, the PDS, as it stood earlier, was widely criticised for its failure to serve the population below the poverty line, its urban bias, negligible coverage in the States with the highest concentration of the rural poor and lack of transparent and accountable arrangements for delivery. Realising this, the Government streamlined the PDS by issuing special cards to families Below Poverty Line (BPL) and selling foodgrains under PDS to them at specially subsidised prices, with effect from June, 1997.

Under the new system, viz., Targeted Public Distribution System (TPDS) the States are required to formulate and implement fool-proof arrangements for identification of poor, for delivery of foodgrains to Fair Price Shops and for its distribution in a transparent and accountable manner at the FPS level. The thrust is to include only the really poor and vulnerable sections of the society such as landless agricultural labourers, marginal farmers, rural artisans/craftsmen such as potters, tappers, weavers, blacksmiths, carpenters, etc. in the rural areas and slum dwellers and persons earning their livelihood on a daily basis in the informal sector like porters, rick-shaw pullers and hand-cart pullers, fruit and flower sellers on the pavements, etc. in urban areas.

Each poor family is entitled to 10 Kg. of foodgrains, per month at specially subsidised prices. The scheme is intended to benefit about 6 crore poor families for whom a quantity of about 72 lakh tonnes of foodgrains is earmarked annually. The identification of the poor is done by the States as per State-wise poverty estimates of Planning Commission based on the methodology of the "Expert Group on estimation of proportion and number of poor" chaired by Late Prof. Lakdawala. The allocation of foodgrains to the States/UTs is made on the basis of average consumption in -the past, i.e., average annual offtake of foodgrains under PDS during the past ten year. The quantum of foodgrains in excess of the requirement of BPL families @ 10kg. per family per month is provided to the States as 'transitory allocation' for which a quantum of 103 lakh tonnes of foodgrains is earmarked annually. This transitory allocation is intended for continuation of benefit of subsidised foodgrains to population above poverty line (APL) as any sudden withdrawal of APL population from the existing PDS was not considered desirable. The transitory allocation is issued at prices which are subsidised but are higher than the prices for BPL quota of foodgrains. The end retail price is fixed by the States/UTs after taking into account margins for wholesalers/retailers, transportation charges, levies, local taxes etc. Under TPDS the States are required to issue foodgrains at a margin of not more than 50 paise per kg. over and above the CIP for

BPL families. For APL families the States can fix the margin keeping in view the actual expenses incurred. The State-wise allocation under TPDS are given in Table-III.

The TPDS has been launched with effect from 1 st June, 1997 in all States/UTs except Delhi and Lakshadweep as the identification of the poor and issue of special cards is still to be completed in these two territories.

A Conference of Chief Ministers was held on 30.9.1997 to review the implementation of TPDS. The general consensus was that the allocations under TPDS may be reviewed, the additional allocations may be issued at APL prices, the allocation at APL prices may not be reduced and the margin admissible to Fair Price Shop dealers may be reviewed.

In view of the difficulties expressed by several States following reduction of allocations under TPDS it was decided to make additional allocations to such States at economic cost of FCI we.f. June, 1997. However, following the deliberations in the Conference of the Chief Ministers it has been decided to issue the additional allocations at APL prices subject to availability of foodgrains in the Central Pool and the constraints of subsidy.

The huge PDS network can play a more meaningful role only if the System translates the macro level self-sufficiency in the foodgrains production achieved by the country, into micro level, i.e., by ensuring availability of food for the poor households with the objective of reducing the number of the undernourished. Targeted Public Distribution System with its focus on the poor is the first step towards this end.

Centrally sponsored schemes for strengthening public distribution system

The following centrally sponsored schemes are being operated for strengthening the PDS infrastructures of States/UTs.

1. Purchase of mobile vans/trucks
2. Construction of godowns

Earlier the scope of the schemes was restricted to 1775 RPDS blocks. Following the introduction of TPDS the scope of the scheme has been extended throughout the country we.f. 1998-99.

Scheme of financial assistance to states for purchase of mobile vans/trucks

The scheme is intended to provide financial assistance to State Governments/UT Administrations for purchase of mobile vans/trucks for distributing essential commodities in rural/hilly/remote and other disadvantaged areas where static/regular fair price shops are not found viable/feasible. Initially an assistance of Rs. 2.50 lakhs was being provided for a delivery van/truck with 75% loan and 25% subsidy. 'With the liberalization of the scheme during 1992-93 the subsidy component of the assistance was enhanced from 25% to 50% and the financial assistance per van/truck was also raised to Rs. 4 lakhs in the case of delivery van (for 4 tonner) and Rs. 8 lakhs for big trucks ranging from 8- 10 tonnes and above subject to the ceiling of actual cost whichever is lower. Under this scheme vehicles can be used not only as mobile fair price shops but can also be used for effecting door delivery of PDS commodities to fair price shops. On the recommendation of working group set up for formulation of 9th plan for PDS, the scope of -the scheme has further been extended to replacement of existing vehicles under the scheme from 1998-99. The scheme is supplementary in nature as the running costs including maintenance are borne by the respective State Governments from their own budget.

Since the inception of the scheme in 1985-86 upto 30.11.1998 a total financial assistance of Rs. 56.54 crores has been provided to 26 States and UTs for purchase of 143, vans/trucks. The outlay for 1998-99 is Rs. 1000 lakhs. Funds under the scheme are released on the basis of utilization of the past assistance by the State Government.

Scheme of financial assistance to states/UTs for construction of godowns

The scheme is intended to assist the State Governments/ UTs for construction of small godowns of the capacity of upto 2000 MTs in interior areas where it is necessary to maintain adequate stocks to ensure regular supplies under PDS. Since 1983-84 this scheme was being implemented to supplement resources of State Governments to augment storage capacity in remote/ inaccessible/hilly areas. Till 1991 the scheme was restricted to North Eastern States, Himachal Pradesh, Sikkim, Jammu & Kashmir, Lakshadweep and Andaman and Nicobar Islands. With the launching of RPDS in January 1992 the scheme was further extended to cover all the identified RPDS areas. Funds under the scheme are released for small godowns where Central agencies like CWC, FCI etc. do not operate. The present pattern of financial assistance is 50% loan and 50% subsidy. However in case of UTs without legislatures the entire assistance is in the form of subsidy only.

Since the inception of scheme in 1983-84 upto 30.11.1998 financial assistance to the extent of Rs. 52.19 crores has been sanctioned for construction of 522 godowns for raising the additional storage capacity of 246642 MTs in 25 States and UTs. The outlay for 1998-99 is Rs. 1250 lakhs. Fresh funds under the scheme are released on the basis of utilization certificate submitted by the State Government for the assistance given to them in previous year (s).

Plan scheme of research, training and monitoring

In addition to the above two schemes and in order to strengthen and upgrade the skills of personnel engaged in the PDS and to improve its management, the Ministry operates a plan scheme for providing financial assistance to State Governments/UT Administrations for training their personnel. The scheme was included in the 6th Five Year Plan. The outlay for the year 1998-99 for this scheme is Rs. 50 lakhs. The following components have been included for financial assistance in the Scheme:

(i) Training Programmes for junior and middle level official of the State Governments/UT Administrations engaged in supply management of essential commodities through PDS.

(ii) Training Programmes for officials of the States/UT Civil Supplies Corporations.

(iii) Seminars/Workshops for senior level officials of the States/UTs engaged in supply management of essential commodities and Central Ministries/ Organizations concerned.

(iv) Research studies on various aspects of PDS.

In the past, 8 research studies have been conducted. Two studies have been commissioned during the year:

(i) Social audit evaluation of Save Grain Campaign scheme.

(ii) Preparation of model for open sale of foodgrains as a measure of market intervention for controlling prices.

The scope of the scheme has been extended from 1998-99 to provide financial assistance to States/UTs for purchase of computer and other ancillary units to link the office of the Director (Civil Supplies) of the respective State Governments with the NIC network. In order to reflect the activities of the scheme suitably, it has been renamed as "Research, Training and Monitoring" during 1998-99. It was earlier named as "Intelligence, Enforcement and Manpower Training".

Open market sale scheme (domestic)

Open sale of wheat and rice is undertaken by the Government through Food Corporation of India As and when considered necessary in order to exert moderating influence on the open market prices of wheat and rice without jeopardising the Public Distribution System.

Food Corporation of India was authorised to sell wheat in the open market in October 1993 and rice in January, 1994 with the following objectives:

i) to release much needed storage space for ensuing procurement season for paddy/rice/wheat;

ii) to reduce the carrying cost of stocks held by Food Corporation of India;

iii) to exercise as a measure of market intervention, a sobering influence on the open market prices of wheat in the coming lean season; and

iv) to reduce to some extent the food subsidy bill.

A quantity of 183.88 lakh tonnes of wheat and 13.61 lakh tonnes of (ice was sold by Food Corporation of India in the open market upto March, 1997. The year-wise break-up of the quantity of wheat and rice sold in the open market is as under:

(Qty. in lakh tonnes)

Year	*Wheat*	*Rice*
1993-94	28.56	0.17
1994-95	50.29	4.54
1995-96	63.38	6.36
1996-97	41.65	2.54

Keeping in view the tight stock position of wheat and rice in the Central Pool, sale of wheat by Food

Corporation of India in the open market was discontinued w.e.f. 1.4.1997.

Subsequently, when there was shortage of wheat and market prices showed in increasing trend, it was decided with the approval of Cabinet Committee on Prices to authorise Food Corporation of India to release 3 lakh tonnes of wheat from January, 1998 to March, 1998 to State Governments as market intervention measure at a price of Rs. 650/- per quintal. A quantity of approx. 31,300 M.T of wheat was lifted under this scheme. Although the offtake of wheat under this scheme has been low it appears to have had a sobering effect on the open market prices of wheat as there was no significant rise in prices of wheat in 1997-98.

In pursuance of the decision of Cabinet Committee on Prices, Govt. has decided to release upto 40 lakh tonnes of wheat to State Governments for open sale at the rates that have been fixed separately for the four Zones in the country. The State Governments have been given the option/choice to release his wheat through PDS outlets or through Roller Flour Mills, Co-op. Agencies and State Govt. Agencies or exercise both the options.

The issue prices of FCI for open sale of wheat are as under:

Name of Zone	*Rate per quintal (in Rs.)*
North Zone	Rs. 653/-
South Zone	Rs. 724/-
West Zone	Rs. 697/-
East Zone	Rs. 716/-

All the State Govts./U.T Administrations have been requested on 18.11.98 to intimate their requirement of wheat under OMSS(D) scheme. The State Govts- of

Maharashtra, Haryana, Karnataka, Orissa, Andhra Pradesh, West Bengal, Gujarat, Kerala, Tamilnadu, Pondicherry, J&K, Chandigarh (U.T), Punjab, Assam and Manipur have responded so far and the work of allotment of wheat to these states under open market sale scheme (domestic) through FCI is in progress.

Government has, however, not undertaken sale of rice in the open market.

Open sale of rice

After attaining a fair degree of success in the open market sale of 'wheat both in terms of augmentation of open market availability and stabilisation of prices, similar efforts were initiated in organising open sale of rice during January, 1994 with the approval of Ministry of Finance.

Open sale of rice was continued in 1995-96 and 1996-97 in all the states on almost similar lines as those of wheat. During 1996-97, FCI was authorised to sell a quantity of 5 lakh tonnes of rice.

The off-take of rice under the scheme has been very low as only a quantity of 0. 17 lakh tonnes was sold during 1993-94, 4.54 lakh tonnes in 1994-95, 6.37 lakh tonnes in 1995-96 and 2.46 lakh tonnes was sold during 1996-97. The sale of rice in the open market was discontinued with effect from 1.4.97.

The reasons for poor off-take of rice under open market sale scheme (domestic) of rice are as under:

i) There is no organised group of buyers of rice in the market as compared to wheat, where All India Federation of Roller Flour Mills with its network all over the country exists.

ii) The rice millers and their Associations also sell rice to the traders and in this way become FCI's competitors.

iii) Good paddy harvest resulting in more availability of rice in the market/with traders.

iv) Lower market prices in states as compared to the prices of open market sale of rice by FCI.

v) Rice of consumers preference is not available with FCI.

vi) The quality of stock with FCI is poor which contained higher broken percentage and admixture.

vii) Generally, old rice was being sold by FCI in 1996-97 under open market sale scheme.

This Ministry has received the approval of Cabinet Committee on Prices (CCP) for disposal of 30 lakh M.T. of rice in the open market for domestic purposes. A close watch is being kept on prices of rice and procurement trend of paddy during the current Kharif season. The Govt. will intervene at appropriate time, if considered necessary. No open sale of rice is, however, being undertaken.

Subsidy on foodgrains to the food corporation of India

The difference between the Food Corporation of India's Economic Cost of foodgrains and the average Sales Realisation is reimbursed to the Corporation by the Central Government as Consumer Subsidy. Since November, 1997 a scheme of decentralised procurement, in the State of West Bengal has been introduced from 1997-98 for supply of Rice to the BPL families. The Government of West Bengal is being reimbursed the difference of Economic cost and the Central Issue Price (CIP) as consumer subsidy through FCI at present. The expenditure incurred by the Food Corporation of India on the maintenance of stocks of foodgrains on behalf of the Central Government is also reimbursed to it as carrying cost of buffer stocks besides the regularised storage and transit shortages. Accordingly, during the current financial year an amount of Rs. 7233.5606 crores (upto January, 1999) has been released to the Food Corporation of India on foodgrains transactions which includes Rs. 45.08 crores paid to the Govt. of West Bengal for decentralised procurement.

Internal movement of foodgrains

Coordinating and monitoring the movement of foodgrains from the surplus areas to the deficit areas vis-a-vis the availability, allocations, offtake and storage capacity is one of the important functions of the Department of Food and Civil Supplies. The Food Corporation of India undertakes activities connected with the movement of foodgrains to the tune of about 20 million tonnes in a year for the Public Distribution System and other welfare schemes. The Movement Division in the Department of Food and Civil Supplies maintains close coordination with the Food Corporation of India, Railways and the various State Governments at the various stages of planning, loading, movement and unloading of foodgrains.

The overall movement of foodgrains during 1998-99 is estimated to be about 17.5 million tonnes as against 19 million tonnes during 1997-98. The reduction is mainly in respect of inter-State movement. About 15 million tonnes of foodgrains are estimated to move on inter-State account during 1998-99. Approximately 92% of the overall movement is expected by rail and the rest by road. During the period April 1998 to November 1998 about 108.84 lakh tonnes of foodgrains were moved by rail and 8.21 lakh tonnes by road as against 121 lakh tonnes by rail and 6.96 lakh tonnes by road during the corresponding period of the previous year. Approximately 13.60 lakh tonnes of imported wheat was moved during April-November, 1998 as against 12.62 lakh tonnes during April-November, 1997.

Improvement in the procurement of foodgrains in the various States, reduction in offtake in many areas and the comfortable stock position of foodgrains in general resulted in reduction in overall movement of foodgrains. Incessant rains and spate of flood in Assam and North Bengal also affected the movement.

Movement ex-north

Approximately 12.5 Broad-Gauge rakes per day were moved ex-North during 1998-99. About 79.63 lakh tonnes of foodgrains were moved during April-November 1998 as against 91.25 lakh tonnes during the corresponding period of the previous year. Movement from other sources, however, increased to 39.12 lakh tonnes as against 36.76 lakh tonnes during the corresponding period of the previous year. Movement ex-North also improved to some extent from August '98. Movement to north-eastern states, Jammu & Kashmir and Himachal Pradesh

As a result of sustained efforts, induction of foodgrains to North-Eastern region improved by 21.5% during April-November, 1998. About 12.34 lakh tonnes of foodgrains were inducted into the North-Eastern region as against 10.26 lakh tonnes during the corresponding period of the previous year.

The winter stocking of Leh and Kargil was completed well before the onset of winter. 3.76 lakh tonnes of foodgrains were inducted in Jammu & Kashmir during April to November, 1998 as against 4.28 lakh tonnes during April-November, 1997. Induction of foodgrains to Himachal Pradesh increased to 1.72 lakh tonnes during April-November, 1998 as against 1.49 lakh tonnes during the corresponding period of previous year.

Movement of the gift consignment of about 20,000 MTs of parboiled non-Basmati rice from the Government of India to the Government of Bangladesh was organised at short notice during October-November, 1998 in coordination with the various agencies and Ministries concerned.

Farm level storage practices

In addition to provide facilities for storage of foodgrains required for buffer and operational needs, with a view to minimise the post harvest losses occuring at farm level, the Dept. of Food Civil Supplies continued its activities to improve the storage practices at farm level at which a major operation of the foodgrains produced is retained for food, feed and seed purposes.

Save grain campaign

The activities under the Save Grain Campaign (SGC) which was launched as a pilot scheme in 1965-66 and being operated as a regular scheme since 1969-70 continued with the objective of disseminating the techniques, of scientific storage of foodgrains to the farming community. The scheme is implemented through a network of 17 SGC offices in close collaboration with the State Govts. The main objective of the scheme is to provide technical knowhow developed by IGMRI to the farmers to minimise the post harvest losses in foodgrains. The major planks of the scheme are training, demonstration and publicity in the selected villages.

Training

During the year under report both stipendiary and non-stipendiary training programmes were conducted. The stipend being paid to the trainee farmers was revised from Rs. 150 to Rs. 250. During 1998-99 (upto November, 1998) 245 stipendiary training programmes were conducted and 12,181 farmers/farm women were trained. Special attention was given to train the farmers belonging to SC/ST and 47 training programmes were organised exclusively for ST community and 2148 farmers/farm women were trained. Besides, 20 training courses for 418 village level workers and 583 training courses for 10905 volunteers were also organised. In addition, SGC offices also collaborated in various training programmes organised by other institution s/agencies and imparted training to 5750 candidates in 57 training courses during the same period.

Demonstration

In order to educate the farmers on scientific storage of foodgrains and post harvest loss minimisation, demonstration on insect and rodent control methods were organised in selected villages and farmers were explained with the recommended storage practices. Improved metallic and nonmetallic storage structures as well as feasible improvements in traditional storage structures were also demonstrated. During 1998-99 (upto November, 1998), 11275 storage receptacles and 103256 rat burrows were fumigated. Rodent control measures in 26773 houses were undertaken and prophylactic treatment in 603 villages covering 14790 storage premise was undertaken. In addition 784 non-metallic storage structures were erected and 9677 indigenous storage structures were improved in the farmers' premises in different villages.

Publicity

In order to make the farmers increasingly aware of the need for the scientific storage of foodgrains, multi-media publicity was organised with particular emphasis on the visual media for which the SGC offices have been provided with demonstration vans equipped with audio-visual aids. The SGC offices arranged 541 exhibitions and 852 film/slides shows during 1998-99 (upto November, 1998). 279 radio talks were broadcast and 28 TV programmes were telecast. The SGC offices also participated in 9 exhibitions/fairs at Regional/State level.

Assistance provided by State Govts./NGOs for popularising scientific storage structures

Since, SGC field offices have limited infrastructure and funds available in order to cover larger number of farmers/ villages, efforts were made to actively involve the State Govts., Non-Governmental organisations, Public Sector Undertakings etc. in the activities of the SGC as a result of which some of the State Govts., viz Madhya Pradesh, Gujarat and Govt. agencies like Project Tiger, Narmada Valley Development Project, Gram Panchayats in Andhra Pradesh, Steel Authority of India Ltd., Indore, Associated Cement Companies Limited, Bhopal and some of the NGOs like Milk Cooperative Society, Anekal, Syndicate Raitha Seva Sahakara Sangh Niyamitha in Karnataka State and. MYRADA PLAN, Shantimalai Trust in Tamil Nadu have provided specific assistance for organising training programmes, supply of metal bins and construction of Pucca Kothi etc.

Development of nucleus in villages

SGC offices are engaged in developing the nucleus villages wherein at least 30% existing storage structures are improved upon and about 10% storage structures are scientific ones like metal bin, pusa bin, pucca kothi and RCC Ring bin. To develop the nucleus villages, assistance for purchasing the metal bins @ Rs.5000/- per village is provided to the farmers for this activity. During this period 225 nucleus villages were developed.

Research & development and institutional training on storage

The Indian Grain Storage Management and Research Institute (IGMRI), Hapur and its five field stations located at Hyderabad, Jabalpur, Jorhat, Ludhiana and Udaipur carried out Research & Development activities on storage and preservation of foodgrains both at farm and commercial level. The Institute also developed code of storage practices for scientific storage of foodgrains which are propagated to the farming community through the Save Grain Campaign network.

The Institutes also conduct long-term and short-term as well as Custom packaged specialised training courses on scientific storage and inspection of foodgrains, pest control technology etc. for the benefit of the officers of storage agencies, pest control operators etc. During the year 1998-99 (upto November, 1998) the Institutes conducted seven training courses and trained 169 candidates from various organisations, 26 short-term training courses were also conducted for 256 candidates.

Under the artisan training courses in which rural artisans are trained for 2 weeks on fabrication of modern storage structures and inputs such as inlet and outlet for improvement of traditional storage structures, during the year 1998-99 (upto November, 1998) four courses were conducted for 80 candidates out of which one course was exclusively conducted for the benefit of 20 tribal youths. During 1998-99 under Annual Action Plan, the following five R&D projects were -undertaken at IGMRIs:

a) Studies on Aflatoxin B contamination in rice stored at commercial level in Saharanpur and Dehradun Districts of U.P.

b) Study on the joint action of Deltamethrin, Malathion and Vitavex on the viability of urad seed in ambient conditions.

c) Study on extent of admixture or other varieties in Durum Wheat at Hoshiarpur District of Punjab.

d) Effect of phosphene at different dosage against Cryptolestes species under cover fumigation.

e) Incidence of microflora in maize during storage at farm level in Gujarat, Rajasthan and Assam.

IGMRI is also engaged in investigating the nature and extent of losses in foodgrains due to various factors under different agro-climatic conditions. Foodgrains samples collected from procurement I centres, storage depots etc. are analysed for physical quality parameters, mycotoxin and pesticidal contamination, During the year 1998-99 (upto November, 1998) 2286 samples were analysed for physical quality parameters, 321 for mycotoxin contamination and 447 for pesticidal residues.

Compendium on work done by IGMRI on foodgrain storage

As a part of the celebration of 50th Anniversary of India's Independence, the IGMRI brought out a compendium entitled "IGMRI-Vision for Grain Storage for 21st Century" compiling the research work undertaken by IGMRI, Hapur and its field stations during 40 years of existence in the field of Post Harvest Management of Foodgrains. Compendium was released by Shri Satyapal Singh Yadav, Hon'ble Minister of State for Food and Consumer Affairs on 17th August, 1998.

Grain specification and inspection

The Government exercises due control over the quality of foodgrains which are procured, stored and distributed by various public agencies in the country. Quality specifications for the grains procured for Central Pool were fixed at the commencement of the Rabi and Kharif procurement season keeping in view the interest of both the producers as well as the consumers and the provisions under the Prevention of Food Adulteration Act/Rules.

However, due to unseasonal rains in some of the major rice producing states during September-October, 1998, the Government, in order to mitigate the hardships to the farmers, extended relaxation in the specification of paddy and resultant rice within the provisions of PFA Act/Rules.

The Quality Control Wings of the Ministry as well as the FCI constantly monitor the quality of foodgrains at the time of procurement, storage and distribution by conducting inspection of procurement centres, storage depots, FPSs etc. During the year (upto November, 1998) the Quality control Officers inspected 308 storage depots, 212 procurement centres, 319, Fair Price Shops, 109 Rail Heads and 109 Rice mills. 2079 samples of foodgrains and wheat products were collected and got analysed for physical and chemical parameters in the Central Grain Analysis Laboratory (CGAL). The CGAL also trained 85 persons on analysis of foodgrains.

Inspection of imported wheat

To monitor the quality of wheat imported from Australia against the contractual specification, joint inspection of wheat which arrived at various Indian ports through 49 vessels (upto November, 1998) was conducted and 421 wheat samples were analysed. The stocks were found conforming to contractual specification.

6

Price Management and Regulation

General price situation

During the first 9 months of 1998-99, barring some abnormal increase in the prices of some food items, the prices of most of the essential commodities have remained at a modest level. The overall availability of essential commodities was, by and large, satisfactory, except in food articles such as vegetables, edible oils and pulses largely due to increasing gap in demand and supply, near stagnation in production and other seasonal factors coupled with unfavourable weather conditions.

Out of the total 447 commodities included in the Wholesale Prices Index Numbers (WPI) (Base 1991-82=100) compiled by the Ministry of Industry, weekly monitoring is being done for 27 essential commodities by the Department of Consumer Affairs and these account for 22.26% of the total weight in the Wholesale Price Index. They include certain primary articles, fuel items and also some manufactured consumer articles In addition to the above, the Department also monitors daily retail prices at selected centres in respect of 12 essential commodities of mass consumption, viz., rice, wheat, gram, arhar, potatoes, onions, tea, sugar, salt, vanaspati, groundnut oil and mustard oil. These 12 essential commodities account for a total weight of 11.18% in the WPI. It is observed that during the current financial year, the rate of inflation in respect of essential commodities increased sharply than the increase of all commodities.

During the previous financial year 1997-98, the rate of inflation hovered in the range of 6.4% to 3.7% by moving between 6.4% in April, 97 to 5.0% in March, 98. The inflation rate *of* 3.7% in August, 97 was the lowest in the past one decade. The current financial year 199899 started with the inflation rate *of* 5.6% in April, 1998 which moved up steadily to 8.4% in November, 98. The increase in the inflation rate during this period was mainly due to abnormal increase in the prices *of* food articles such as pulses, vegetables and edible oils. However, as a result of the timely measures taken by the Government to control the prices, the inflation rate has moved down to 6.5% in the month of December, 98.

A comparative trend in the annual rates of inflation during the last 4 years is given in the Table below and ii Graph II:-

Table

Annual rate of inflation (in percentage)

Months	*1995-96*	*1996-97*	*1997-98*	*1998-99*
April	10.0	5.0	6.4	5.6
May	9.9	4.5	5.8	6.6
June	9.1	4.5	5.9	7.3
July	8.4	6.0	4.1	8.3
August	8.8	6.2	3.7	8.3
September	8.9	6.5	3.9	8.3
October	8.4	6.6	4.4	8.3
November	8.4	6.5	3.9	8.4
December	6.4	7.5	4.5	6.5
January	5.0	7.5	5.8	
February	4.6	7.9	4.9	
March	5.1	7.1	5.0	

Trend in the prices of some of the selected essential commodities/sub-groups is explained below:

Cereals

(a) The price index of cereals, as a sub-group, increased by 11.5% during the first 9 months of 1998-99. This was mainly attributed to hike in the WPI of rice (13.4%), wheat (9.4%) as well as coarse cereals such as jowar (7.0%), bajra (5.2%), maize (15.3 %), ragi (16.2%) and barley (I. I%).

Pulses

(b) Inspite of a decline of 3.4% in the prices of the WPI of sub-group of pulses increased by 16.3% during April December, 98 on account of increase in the prices of all other pulses in the range of 10.2% (moong) to 45.8% (arhar). The increase in the WPI of masur and urad was to the ex 26.8% and 14.6% during the period under review

Sugar, Khandsari and gur

(c) The WPI of the sub-group of sweetening agents viz. sugar, khandsari and gur, recorded a modest decline of 2.7% during the first 9 months of the current financial year. This was mainly attributed to decline in the price index of gur by 6.4%.' The WPI of sugar and khanasari however, increased at a marginal rate of 0.8% and 1.5% during this period.

Edible oils

(d) The prices of edible oils, as a sub-group, exhibited a sharp rise of 16.8% during the first 9 months of 1998-99. Except a slight increase of 0.3% i vanaspati and 0.4% in cocount oil, the prices of a other major edible oils rose during this period, i the range of 12.4% (groundnut oil) to 60.0 ~mustard oil). This was attributed mainly to decline in production, ban imposed by some States in the sale of mustrad oil in loose due to adultration an, also the existing gap of nearly 12-14 lakh tonnes i demand and supply.

Vegetables

(e) The WPI of vegetable, as a sub-group, rose significantly by 76.5% during the first 9 months of current financial year mainly because of an increase in the prices of onions and potatoes by 119.8% and 89.5% respectively. Seasonal factors play a significant role in the prices of vegetables. Production of onions and potatoes declined substantially during the current year due to unfavourable weather condition. The unseasonal rains coupled with severe spell of summer caused damage to the standing crops resulting in acute shortage of the commodity. However, of late the prices of most of the vegetables have started declining and is now ruling at normal levels.

The percentage variations in the wholesale price indices of selected essential commodities during the month of December, 1998 and in the corresponding period in 1997.

Retail prices

The variation in the wholesale prices of various commodities generally gets-reflected at the retail level also but with a time lag. This variation and the time lag depend on different factors such as market imperfection, movement constraints, stock position, purchasing power etc. and could differ from commodity to commodity. Therefore, the rate of change in the wholesale prices may differ with that at the retail price levels at any particular point of time, because of which it would be difficult to derive any definite conclusion on their parallel movements. However, during the current year, the retail prices of selected essential commodities in various centres across the country moved, by and large, in narrow and reasonable ranges.

Consumer price index

The Consumer Price Index (CPI) number for Industrial Workers, generally reflects the price trend at the retail level. During the first 8 months of 1998-99 (April-November, 1998), the CPI for Industrial Workers rose at a higher rate of 15.3% as compared to a low increase of 4.3% during the corresponding months of 1997-98.

Conclusion

In brief, the prices of most of the food items during the current financial year rose at an abnormal rate while other commodities in the manufacturing sector increased at reasonable rate. Government has given the highest priority for the control of price rise the country. The price situation is reviewed regularly by HPPMB (erstwhile SACP) and CCP. Imports of commodities like pulses, edible oils, etc. are being done to augment their availability on the open market. Import of pulses have been placed under OGL. Import duty on edible oils has been reduced from 25% to 15% w.e.f. 10.7.98. The 4% additional import duty on edible oils used for vanaspati has been abolished w.e.f. 31.10.98. Market intervention was initiated for supply of onion at a subsidised price of Rs. 10.00 per kg. in Delhi we.f. 14.7.98. The scheme was discontinued w.e.f. 1.1.99 as the prices of onions were returned to normal levels. The export of onions has been banned from 14.10.98.

In pursuance of a decision taken by the Prime Minister in a meeting with the Group of Ministers, the Cabinet Secretary held a meeting on November, 7, 1998 with the Chief Secretaries of State Governments and UTs to review the situation arising out of the increase in the prices of some essential commodities. The meeting took note of the abnormal increase in prices and discussed measures, both short term and otherwise, to bring down prices and avoid a recurrence of the problem. The Prime Minister convened a meeting of the Chief Ministers of States and UTs on November 27, 1998 to strengthen the on going efforts of the Government to augment supplies and to stabilise prices. There were useful discussions on a wide range of issues covering various aspects relating to availability, distribution and prices of essential commodities. Valuable suggestions were made during the course of deliberations for adoption of comprehensive measures for stimulating production of essential commodities, protection of the interests of the farmers, institution of proper mechanisms for forecasting of production, monitoring of prices, steamlining of distribution, setting up of cold storage chains and processing facilities, strengthening of Essential Commodities Act and Prevention of Blackmarketing and Maintenance of Supplies of Essential Commodities Act, enforcement of these statutes, etc.

The annual rate of inflation based on the WPI for all commodities is estimated lower at 5% as on 2.1.99 as against 5.6% during the corresponding period of 1997. The prices and availability of essential commodities are being monitored 'by the Ministry regularly on daily and weekly basis and ;suitable measures are taken to avoid shortages and check price rise. Estimates of production of foodgrains, stock of 'cereals in central pool and availability and prices of important ~essential commodities is given below.

Estimates of foodgrains production

(million tonnes)

	Years			*%variation 1997-98*	
Commodity	*1994-95*	*1995-96*	*1996-97*	*1997-98*	*1996-97*
(a) cereals					
Rice	81.81	76.98	81.31	82.12	1.00

Wheat	65.77	62.10	69.27	66.05	-4.65
Jawar	8.97	9.33	11.09	8.33	-24.89
Bajra	7.16	5.38	7.91	7.64	-3.62
Maize	8.83	9.53	10.61	11.09	4.52
Barley	1.73	1.51	1.44	1.67	15 97
Ragi	2.34	2.50	2.47	2.21	-10.53
Small millets	0.80	0.78	0.76	0.66	-13.16
Total	177.46	168.11	184.86	179.97	-2.75
(b) Pulses					
Gram	6.44	4.98	5.76	6.20	7.64
Tur	2.14	2.31	2.70	2.04	-24.44
Other Pulses	5.46	5.02	6.00	5.11	-14..83
Total	14.04	12.31	14.46	13.35	-7.68
Total Foodgrains	191.50	180.42	199.32	193.12	-3.19

Source: Directorate of Economics and Statistics, Ministry of Agriculture.

Stocks cereals in central pools

(Million tonnes)

As on	*Rice*	*Wheat*	*Coarse-grains*	*Total*
1. 1.99(P)	11.68	12.70	0.00	24.38
1. 1.98(P)	11.48	6.76	0.00	18.24
1. 1.97(P)	12.94	7.08	0.00	20.02

Cereals

The total stock of cereal foodgrains in the Central Pool of the Government as on 1.1.99 was 24.38 million tonnes, which was higher than that of 18.24 million tonnes in the corresponding period of the last year. The present foodgrain stock are about 7.58 million tonnes higher than the total minimum stock of 16.80 million tonnes required to be maintained (as on I ' -1.99) by the public agencies under the Buffer Stocking norms.

Rice

The production of rice during the last four years (199495 to .1997-98) has been hovering in the region of around 80-82 million tonnes. For 1997-98 about 82 million tonnes of production of rice has been estimated. The procurement of rice for the central pool has been higher at 143 lakh tonnes in the marketing year 1997-98 as against 122 lakh tonnes procured during 1996-97. Procurement season for 1998-99 marketing year was advanced by a fortnight and commenced from 15.9.98. Upto 20.1.99, 71 lakh tonnes of rice has been procured compaired to 85 lakh tonnes procured during corresponding period last year. The Physical stock of rice in the Central Pool as on 1.1.99 stood at 116.83 lakh tonnes which was higher by 32.83 lakh tonnes than the stock required to be maintained as on 1.1.99 under Buffer Stock norms. During 1998 a quantity of 125.49 lakh tonnes of rice has been allocated for distribution under PDS as against 135.14 lakh tonnes allocated during last year. The off-take of rice during calender year 1997 stood at 102.43 lakh tonnes (76% of allocation). The off-take of rice during 1998 stood at 103.73 lakh tonnes which is about 82% of allocation. Availability of rice in the open market remained comfortable and prices remained stable during the year.

Wheat

The production of wheat has been estimated at 66.05 million tonnes in 1997-98 against the target of 68.50 lakh tonnes. Production of wheat during 1996-97 was 69.27 million tonnes. The stock of wheat in central pool as on 1.1.99 was 127.0 lakh tonnes which is higher than the minimum stock of 84 lakh tonnes required under the Buffer Stocking norms as on 1. 1.99. In order to maintain adequate supply of wheat in the country and also to replensh the significant drawdown of stocks last year the

STC was authorised to import 1.5 million tonnes of wheat during 1998-99. To contain the prices of wheat and atta in the open market the roller flour mills are allowed to import their wheat requirements under OGL through registration with APEDA. Availability of wheat in the open market remained comfortable and prices remained stable during the year.

Pulses

The production of pulses in the country have been stagnating at 12-14 million tonnes. For many years. The production of pulses during 1997-98 has been estimated at 13.35 million tonnes, which is 7.7%. lower than the level achieved during 1996-97. The gap between demand and supply of pulses in the country is estimated over 2 million tonnes. To augment supplies of pulses their import is placed under OGL and import duty on pulses was abolished to further improve their availability in the country. During 1998-99, 2.09 lakh tonnes of pulses were imported upto Nov. 98 as against import of 6.15 lakh tonnes during corresponding period last year. Availability of pulses in the open market was comfortable, however, due to unbridged gap of demand and supply prices of pulses remained under pressure during the year.

Edidle oils

There is a gap of about 14 lakh tonnes in demand and supply of edible oils in the country which is to be met from imports. During 1998-99, 17.11 lakh tonnes of edible oils was imported upto Nov. 98 as compared to import of 10.32 lakh tonnes during corresponding period of last year. The total import of edible oil during 1997-98 was 11.3 lakh tonnes as against 14.16 lakh tonnes for 1996-97. The Government imported 1.5 lakh tonnes of RBD palmolein through STC during the year for distribution through PDS. To augment supply of edible oils in the country Government reduced import duty on edible oils from 25% to 15% during the year. Because of unbridged gap between demand and supply the prices of edible oils remained under pressure during the year. Cases of adulteration of mustard oil reported from some places especially from Delhi disrupted supplies of mustard oil during Sept. & Oct. 98 and many State Governments banned sale of mustard oil during these months.

Sugar

The prices and supply position of sugar has remained satisfactory during the year. During the sugar year 1997-98 the production of sugar was estimated at 128.27 lakh tonnes which is almost at the same level of 128.46 lakh tonnes during 1996-97 sugar year. During the sugar year 1997-98 (Oct.-Sept.) 138.68 lakh tonnes of free sale and levy sugar was released for distribution through PDS. The sugar stock was 61.25 lakh tonnes as on 31.12.98 as against 64.81 lakh tonnes during the corresponding period last year. The availability of sugar is comfortable in open market and prices of sugar also remained stable during the year.

Vegetables

The prices of vegetables showed abnormal increase's during the year due to decline in production and crop damages because of adverse climatic conditions. The increase in prices was very high particularly of onions. To augment supplies of Onions Government has banned export of onions, abolished import duty on onions and placed its import under OGL. The Department of Consumer Affairs also initiated action to supply onions at subsidised rate of Rs. 10/- Kg through Public Distribution Agencies at Delhi from 14.7.98.

Tea

The availability position of tea in the open market was

satisfactory and prices also remained stable during the year The production of tea for the year 1998 was estimated higher at 867 million kg. as against 811 million kg. during 1997.

Salt

The availability of salt remained satisfactory throughout the year in the country except for a few days towards end (Oct. and beginning of Nov. 1998 when rumour inspired report of shortage of salt were received from some States/UTs such as Delhi, Bihar, UP. Secretary '(Consumer Affair: immediately convened a meeting of popular manufacture of salt to ensure its availability and adequate publicity about availability of sufficient stock 6f salt in the country was also given to ward off rumours.

Essential commodities act, 1955

The Essential Commodities Act, 1955 was enacted to ensure easy availability of essential commodities to consumers and to protect them from exploitation by traders. The Act provides for regulation and control of production, distribution and pricing of commodities which are declared as essential under the Act. Presently there are 31 classes of commodities which are declared essential under the Act. The Act was amended from time to time to make its provisions more effective. In order to create greater impact on the defaulting traders, the provisions of the Essential Commodities Act, 1955 were made more stringent making the offences non-bailable and providing for summary trial of such offences by Special Courts through the Essential Commodities (Special Provisions) Act, 1981, the validity of which had been extended upto 31st August, 1997 on the basis of unanimous recommendations of the States/UT Governments.

The Essential Commodities (Special Provisions) Bill,

1997 was introduced in Lok Sabha on 1.8.97 to extend Essential Commodities (Special Provisions) Act, 1981 for a further period of five years. The said Bill lapsed on dissolution of the Lok Sabha. There-after, two Essential Commodities (Special Provisions) Ordinances were promulgated on 3.10.97 and 2.1.98 on the lines of 1997 Bill alongwith certain amendments. In pursuance of the recommendations of the Expert Group constituted by Deptt. of Consumer Affairs, it was decided to incorporate the provisions of Essential Commodities (Special Provisions) Act in the Essential Commodities Act on permanent basis alongwith certain changes. Accordingly, the Essential Commodities (Amendment) Ordinance was issued on 25.4.98 followed by introduction of Essential Commodities (Amendment) Bill, 1998 in Lok Sabha on 29.5.98. The Bill was referred to the Standing Committee of Parliament which in its report dated 26.6.98 suggested a few changes. Thereafter, the Bill was referred to the Joint Parliamentary Committee on 9.7.98. The Committee has now regretted its inability to give any report within the time granted. In the meantime, the Ordinance dated 25.4.98 lapsed.

In pursuance of the decision taken in the Conference of Chief Ministers of States/UTs held on 27,11.98 under the chairmanship of the Prime Minister, a Group of Officers was constituted under the chairmanship of the Cabinet Secretary. The State Governments of West Bengal, Rajasthan, Maharashtra and Andhra Pradesh were represented on the Group. The meeting of the Group was held on 8.12.98. The Group in its report has recommended modification of certain provisions of the Essential Commodities (Amendment) Bill, 1998 so as to make it more deterrent and effective. On the basis of the recommendations of the Group of Officers it has been decided to introduce in the Parliament a revised Essential

Commodities (Amendment) Bill, 1999 for modifying some of the proposals of the Essential Commodities (Amendment) Bill, 1998.

The Central Government is regularly monitoring the action taken by State Govts./UT Administrations to implement the provisions of the Essential Commodities Act, 1955. The action taken by States/UTs under the Act during the year 1998 (reported upto 31.12.98) is as indicated below:-

i)	No. of raids made	62433
ii)	No. of persons arrested	5033
iii)	No. of persons prosecuted	4606
iv)	No. of persons convicted	3700
v)	Value of goods confiscated	2208.57 (in lakhs)

Prevention of blackmarketing and maintenance of supplies of essential commodities act, 1980

In order to prevent unethical trade practices like hoarding and blackmarketing etc. the Prevention of Blackmarketing and maintenance of Supplies of Essential Commodities Act, 1980 is being implemented by the State Govts/UT Administrations. The Act empowers the Central and State Govts. to detain persons whose activities are found to be prejudicial to the maintenance of supplies of commodities essential to the community. The number of persons ordered to be detained under the Act in various States/UTs during the year 1998 was 131.

7

Harvesting Season

There are three main crop seasons in our country namely, kharif, rabi and summer. Major kharif crops are rice, jowar, bajra, maize, cotton, sugarcane, sesame, soyabean and groundnut. Major rabi crops are wheat, jowar, barley, gram, linseed, rapeseed and mustard. Rice, maize and groundnut are grown in summer season also.

Land utilisation statistics are available for 92.8 per cent of total geographical area of 3,287.3 lakh hectare. According to land use statistics available from states, area under forests had increased from 404.8 lakh hectare in 1950-51 to 680.2 lakh hectare in 1992-92. Net sown area increased from 1,187.5 lakh to 1,414.1 lakh hectare during the same period. Broad cropping pattern indicates that though foodgrains, their relative share came down from 76.7 per cent during 1950-51 to 67.2 per cent during 1991-92.

Overall economic growth in terms of Gross Domestic Product (GDP) at constant factor cost improved from 0.8% in 1991-92 to 6.3% in 1994-95 and 7% in 1995-96 aided by a growth rate of 2.4% by agriculture and allied sectors, 11.7% by industry and construction sector and 7% by services. Overall economic growth during the first four year of the 8th Plan (1992-97) averaged 5.9% per annum compared with the planned target of 5.6%.

The domestic savings rate measured in terms of gross domestic savings as a proportion of GDP at current market prices increased from an average rate of 21.3% in 1992-93 and 1993-94 to 24.4% in 1994-95. The rate of domestic investment measured in terms of gross domestic capital formation as a proportion of GDP at current market prices increased from 21.6% in 1993-94 to 25.2% in 1994-95.

Industrial production which was virtually stagnant in 1991-92 increased by 9.4% and 12.1% in 1995-96 supported by a growth rate of 6.9% in mining, 13.6% in manufacturing and 8.1% in electricity generation. As per the latest information available, industrial growth deceleration to 8.5% in April-June 1996 due to deceleration of growth rates in all the sub-sectors (3.6% in mining, 10.4% manufacturing and 2.2% in electricity generation). As per growth rates by use-based classification, capital goods sector recorded a growth rate of 14.2%, intermediate goods 11.9%, consumer durables 11.1% and consumer non-durables 8.6% in April-June 1996. However, the growth rate of basic goods sub-sector having a weight of 39.4% in the overall industrial production was only 4% in April-June 1996.

Seven infrastructural sectors, namely, electricity, coal, steel, cement, crude oil and petroleum product & fertilizer with a combined weight of 31% in the Index of Industrial Production (IIP) recorded a growth rate of 7.8% in 1995-96. But their growth rate decelerated to 3.2% in April-August 1996 due to poor performance of electricity generation (growth rate of only 2.4%) and crude oil production (decline of production by 10.4%).

The outlook of agricultural production in 1996-97 is excellent with foodgrains output likely to reach 197 million tonnes compared with 185 million tonnes in 1995-96. This is primarily due to this year's rainfall distribution being the best in the past five years. The late withdrawal of monsoon has further ensured bright prospects for rabi production this year. The estimate of foodgrains production in 1995-96 has been scaled down to 185 million tonnes representing a sharp decline of nearly 6 million tonnes over the preceeding year. The shortfall was substantial (about 3 million tonnes) in wheat output, besides short-fall of production of rice and coarse cereals. Consequently wheat procurement dropped steeply to 8.2 million tonnes compared to 12.3 million tonnes in the preceding year. Public stock (Central Pool) of foodgrains was about 22.1 million tonnes as on September 1, 1996.

Challenge of hunger

The life and vitality of human beings depend crucially on certain vitamins and minerals that help in the efficient functioning of the brain, immune system, reproduction and energy metabolism. The body needs only small amounts of these nutrients, but it cannot synthesize them. They must be provided through diet. Deficiencies of even the small amounts required cause learning disabilities, impair work capacity and bring illness and death. Micronutrient malnutrition (silent hunger) is most devastating for pre—school children and pregnant women but is also debilitating for all ages. And it is debilitating the national economy as well. The most important and well studied micro-nutrient deficiencies are vitamin A, Iodine and Iron. Virtually every developing country has deficiencies in the micro nutrients large enough to constitute a public health problem. Many developing countries have multiple deficiencies. Taken together micronutrient deficiencies affect a far greater number of people in the world than Protein-Energy malnutrition. 1.6 billion people live in areas where soils lack sufficient iodine, 655 million suffer from goitre, 26 million have had brain damage and 5.7 million cretinism. Two billion pre-school children suffer from iron deficinet anaemia. 254 million pre-school children are affected by subclinical, severe and moderate deficiencies of Vitamin A.

In India, 167 millions are exposed to the risk of Iodine deficiency of which 54 million have goitre. Surveys conducted by DGHS indicate that 186 districts are IDD endemic area with goitre rates over 10 per cent. As regards Iron deficiency anaemia, multicentre study conducted by ICMR reveal that 87.5 per cent were anaemic. Deficiency of Vitamin A has long been known to be the largest preventable cause of blindness.

The main intervention strategies against micronutrient malnutrition are:

— Diet supplementation of vulnerable population.

— Dietary improvements.

— Fortification of common foods.

The richest sources of micronutrients are green leafy vegetable and fruits. India is rich in vegetable crops, some of which have good carotene content. Future programmes with respect to horticultural products must be directed towards identifying and propagating high micro-nutrient concentration varieties. People know when they are hungry but they have no natural hunger for vitamin. A, Iron, Iodine and other micronutrients. They do not know they need them and they often do not know what foods provide them.

Deficiency in soil nutrients reflect in the plants grown in the soil. One—half of all soils in all developing countries are deficient or low in available micronutrients. Soil depletion of S, Fe, Mn, Zn and Cu are due to intensive and indiscriminate irrigation and heavy use of high analysis chemical fertilisers. This gets reflected in the plants grown in these soils. Hence, in the national soil health care programme, we should ensure that both the macro-and micro-nutrient needs of soils are addressed.

The grim crisis, including a farmers' strike, over wheat procurement in Punjab and Haryana despite a hefty 25 per cent increase in purchase prices in a single year highlights the deep trouble brewing in our food economy. Already, the wheat buffer stock has plummeted to an alarming 2.7 million tonnes (mt), well below the recommended minimum of 3.7 mt, down from 12.9 mt just two years ago. Everything that the government has dome in the 1990s—from exporting grain when world prices are low, and importing when high, to raising procurement and issue prices unconscionably—speaks of gross mismanagement. If this continues, we could soon have Pakistan-style food riots. Already, the spectre of starvation and severe undernourishment stalks parts of Orissa, Maharashtra, Madhya Pradesh and Rajasthan. Our creaking public distribution system and its "targeted" variant, is in danger of collapsing. And yet there is irresponsible talk in policy circles of "unshackling" non-basmati rice exports and aligning domestic input and output prices with international levels.

That our food security should have been so badly undermined despite nine consecutive good monsoons speaks of a deep policy malaise and official callousness. The nineties have seen, for the first time in nearly four decades, foodgrain output growth lagging behind populaltion growth. Output growth has decelerated to less than half the 3.5 per cent rate of the 1980s. The slowdown is particularly severe in the case of rice and wheat, where the states that hold the key to marketable surpluses—and account for 80 per cent-plus of procurement—have witnessed a fall in growth rates to just 0.9 and 1.6 per cent, i.e. well below the population growth rate of 1.9 per cent. In our largest grain-producing state, paddy and wheat yields have fallen by 12 and 10 per cent respectively since 1992. Meanwhile, the output of "coarse" Meanwhile, the output of "coarse" cereals and pulses continues to shrink, eroding the food base of the poor, even as real farm wages decline.

Evidently, 30 years after it was launched, the Green Revolution has run its course or exhausted its potential, especially in the agriculturally most advanced areas. Northwestern India and parts of Andhra and Tamil Nadu show a clear trend of yields and output falling despite significant additions of inputs such as chemical fertiliser. Although eastern India has done relatively better, it simply can not compensate for the decline in the granary-states. In India as a whole, there are steeply falling returns to investment and inputs. As land is increasingly diverted to non-foodgrain uses, grain availability is further threatened. Given declining public investment in agriculture,—all this spells serious food insecurity.

Why has this happened? There are several reasons. First and foremost, the Green Revolution has come up against ecological and natural resources barriers. Its classic "package of practices" —high-yield (really high-response) seeds, big doses of irrigation, fertilisers and pesticides—backed by loans and guaranteed prices, is simply not sustainable in a natural-resources-poor society. In Punjab, 85 per cent of land has no more groundwater left to exploit. In Haryana, water-logging and salinity affect nearly a third of all land. In UP and Andhra, an overdose of chemicals is playing havoc with soil fertility. Farmers, who have oversaturated and killed lands with toxic chemicals, are now turning to nitrogen-fixing *dhancha* plants.

Secondly, unbalanced fertiliser use—encouraged by

the Rs. 9,300 crore subsidy for urea—is playing havoc with soil health. The nitrogen-phosphorus-potassium ratio has changed to 8.5:6.6:1 in place of the optimal 4:2:1. (In UP, it is a dangerous 30:6:1). There is a severe and growing scarcity of micronutrients like zinc, copper, iron and manganese. A National Academy of Agricultural Sciences report warms of grave danger if micronutrients are not replenished and green-manuring not practised. Fertiliser overuse has been economically counterproductive too. Thus, fertiliser consumption has increased eight times over the past 25 years, but foodgrains output has not even doubled.

Third, the Green revolution's genetic breakthrough was largely limited to wheat and rice, which official policy favoured, while ignoring "coarse" grains)in reality, highly nutritious millets consumed by the poor). The result has been growing monocultures of rice and wheat, and loss of biodiversity. This also means inappropriate land-use: Punjab and Haryana, whose climate is unconducive to rice, have become its major producers. The Gangetic plains have turned into an environmentally unsustainable rice-wheat cropping system. Another consequence is sub-optimal use of water, and overuse of power, neither of which we can afford: the capital cost of major irrigation today is of the order of Rs. 50-80,000 per hectare. Servicing this annually alone would wipe out all profit from agriculture if the farmer were to bear the cost. He doesn't. The state does.

Fourth, in the nineties, the government deliberately changed its earlier policy of trying to keep food prices low. Following the premise that high output prices, and subsidised inputs would attract more investment and make agriculture competitive, it more than doubled the fertiliser subsidy. The idea was to "globalise" domestic prices for a specific crop spurt investment into its cultivation, but the aggregate supply response to an across-the-board increase in output prices is very weak. Hence prices have risen, but investment, yield and output have not.

These processes/factors have resulted in a first-rate agrarian crisis. This crisis cannot be resolved by adding inputs, or promoting better fertiliser/pesticide use—i.e. more of the same. Dying land which has less then two per cent organic matter left in it cannot be revived by chemical means. There is no way that our electrical system can support the current 10-12 per cent annual increase in power consumption which water-intensive agriculture demands.

A paradigm shift is on order. we need a "Doubly Green revolution", which judiciously uses advances in plant genetics and biotechnology, but is simultaneously resource conserving and environmentally sound. This means a transition from high-energy, chemical-and water-intensive agriculture to low-input, low-chemical, more organic, waterconserving farming. It means altering the direction of breeding towards sturdy, drought-and-pest-resistant seeds based on indigenous genetic material and away from rice and wheat to millets, pulses and grasses. It means moving away from monocultures to plural agri-silvi-pastoral systems which recycle biomass. It means conserving energy. It means moving from big to small farmers.

Fortunately, we have a highly evolved agricultural research-and-extension system with the resources to undertake this transition. We must strengthen it, and discourage capital-and energy-intensive seed-breeding based on exogenous material. We must abandon the chimerical goal of "globalisation" and look at our own needs, endowments and knowledge systems. Such a paradigm shift alone can resolve today agrarian crisis.

New Delhi: If you live in the cities of India what you mostly hear about is what you haven't got but should be trying to: a better job perhaps your own flat, a new vehicle, or may be a credit card or a cell phone. Only now and again your eye may fall on newspaper stories about the wheat shortage or, if you are listening hard enough loud the rising prices and terrible shortage of atta in the market. You don't have to be a professional economist to tell that something must be very wrong if there is a foodgrain shortage after being repeatedly told that the country actually exports wheat, and also after hearing the Prime Minister's back-thumping sermon about India's self-sufficiency at the World Food Summit in Rome last month.

A couple of shocking statistics, recently released by the National Council of Applied Economic Research (NCAER) provide a horrific, if more accurate picture of where we are. The first figure is that 39 per cent of India's population of nearly one billion remains under the poverty line, a number that hasn't changed in a decade. In real terms this means that a very large number of Indians have an earning capacity of Rs. 5 or less a day, and are lucky to scratch up a meal of a couple of *chappatis*. According to another survey by the NCAER, 37 per cent of the country's rural population is landless and therefore unable to grow their own crop to fend off hunger.

The second figure, less published but available from international agencies, is that foodgrain production has been declining despite good monsoons—overall from 191 million tonne in 1994-95 to 185 million tonne in 1995-96 and in the case of wheat, from 65.5 million tonne to 62.6 million tonne in the same period. Unsurprisingly, the worst production shortfalls are in the politically volatile states of Uttar Pradesh and Bihar. Yet the naked face of hunger continues to be masked by the hypocrisy that India is an foodgrain exporter.

Still, there are plenty of Indians who want to know not merely how the government is in a position to export several million tonnes of wheat when there isn't enough to feed to the hungry, and then, to start importing two million tonnes to fill the ration shops when a widespread scarcity arises and prices begin to shoot up. A leader in The Economic Times last week argues that the government, the largest hoarder of foodgrains in the country, "is releasing large quantities in the country but not large enough quantities". It makes a strong claim for wheat imports to be put under Open General Licence amidst widespread speculation that the wheat shortage may be a repeat of last year's sugar scam and that the politicians could be back in the import-export business.

Even, if that is not the case, the situation is morally as indefensible as the problem of Indian children in labour—anywhere between 30 to 90 million depending on how you define "labour"—that the Supreme Court recently sought to curtail through stringent penalties. Surely the main reason why millions of our children are in bondage is to escape hunger?

Apart from the rising population, agro-economists put forward a number of reasons for falling production in foodgrains, among them soil exhaustion and the large number of landless that are concentrated in the states of UP, Bihar and eastern India. What they do not spell out is the endemic political instability and corruption in these states, and the interminable cycle of fodder scams and casts wars, that are pushing the poor deeper into the poverty trap. Economic reports do not point out that the agriculture ministry for many years has been managed by ministers like Devi Lal and Balram Jakhar, who only represent the narrow interests of wealthy landed farmers like themselves, and have no truck with the poor landless peasant. Devi Lal is chiefly remembered today for turning his ministerial bungalow and the Ashoka Hotel into a farmer's retreat while Balram Jakhar is the only ember of the PV Narsimha Rao's government involved inboth the *hawala* and *gawala* scams. It cost men like Jakahar nothing to proclaim that India should export pulses apart from wheat, knowing full well that production of pulses was dropping faster than that of wheat. The Deve Gowda government is heir to the same hypocrisy. The Prime Minister wants to impress the world about India's prestige as a wheat exporter but can do nothing about the gnawing pangs of hunger at home. Persisting shortages of food and soaring pricelines are not the result of natural causes alone. They are crises created by the men at the top.

Thirty years ago the Kalahandi region of Orissa had suffered a severe drought causing nearly a thousand deaths due to starvation and related diseases. The number of reported cases of starvation deaths in the current drought in the same area of Western Orissa may not exceed a dozen so far, but the magnitude of the crisis remains almost the same. Vulnerability of the people of this rainshadow area to crop loss and its consequences has hardly changed. Despite the visits of every Prime Minister of India, from Mrs Indira Gandhi to Mr H.D. Deve Gowda, to sypathise with the people and announce new projects, the basic conditions of poverty and underdevelopment have not changed.

Every 10 years there has been a severe drought and every third or fifth year has been a hard-hitting year of agricultural failure. Distress migration in mass scale, sale of household possessions and cattle and, condition of near starvation have been recurring in this region. In fact, as many as 26 out of Orissa's 30 districts have experienced over 50 per cent have experienced over 50 per cent crop loss this year and have been declared drought affected. The Kalahandi experience is a clear indictment of India's development path whether before or after liberalisation.

Failure of rains in the critical post-sowing months of June and July led to crop failure in this region. During My-October 1996 the recorded rainfall was only 632 mm against the average of 1217 mm. It is the erratic nature of the rainfall rather than its absence which upsets the farming process most of the time. The sprouts of paddy as usual dried up in June-July last year. While the traditional sources of water supply have disappeared new irrigation facilities have not sprung up. The worst affected districts of Bolangir and Nuapada (until recently a part of Kalahandi) are strewn with rivers and rivulets which overflow during the rainy season. They carry water into Mahanadi whose basin suffers from floods in the coastral area of Orissa practically every year.

Earlier people had their community tanks, bunds and small barrages to block river water. Slowly the affluent families and government established their control over these lands and used them for other purposes. Over the years community tanks went dry due to lack of public care. Currently only a small portion of cultivable land is irrigated by a few small reservoirs and lift irrigation projects.

During the past two decades the drinking water supply has considerably improved with the installation of tube wells. Even then visitors would see streams of women going to rivers to collect pots of water strained through sand as river water in this region tastes sweeter than underground water. People of the area have been demanding a number of small reservoirs from rivers and streams which would save rain water and tanks in specific spots in the area. this should be supplemented by deep borewells in some places. Lifting water from rivers and tanks through pumps should also be systematically arranged. In fact, an organisation called Sahavagi Vikas Abhijan has made a panchayat-wise study of the irrigation proposals made by the people.

In six blocks of Kalahandi-Nuapara region, which are chronically droughtprone, it has suggested 795 such projects, which would cost approximately Rs. 1,540 crore with a command area of nearly 1,15,000 hectares.

Very little has been done to chalk out a long-term strategy demanded by the people. The much trotted KBK (Longterm Action Plan for Kalahandi Bolangir Koraput region), formulated on the initiative of the PMO in 1993, put all the existing schemes and their allocations together for a five-year period amounting to nearly Rs. 5,000 crore. It is a point of ridicule in the eyes of the public and also the administration since it neither provides additional resources nor addresses the basic causes of the recurring crisis.

There has been some awakening—however marginal it may be among the people. In recent weeks there have been block office gheraos and rasta roko campaigns by people in some places demanding long-term measures to prevent recurrence of drought. Hopefully, the newly elected panchayat leaders will join the stream of awareness growing among the people of the region to carry on a new struggle for the basic human right to a livelihood. Experience shows that when people assert their right to control and utilise their resources then state and capital wake up to negotiate with them.

The term Green Revolution was coined by Dr. William Gadd of USA in 1968, when our farmers brought about a quantum jump in wheat production by taking to semi-dwarf, non-lodging varieties with great enthusiasm and when similar progress appeared feasible in rice. Punjab took the lead because of the scientific and educational backstopping given by the Punjab Agricultural University on the one hand and on the other, by the presence of the essential pre-requisites for progress such as land consolidation and leveling, rural communication, rural electrification and above all, owner cultivation.

Twenty eight years after the term "Green Revolution" was coined, we are in a position to draw a balance sheet and chalk out a strategy for the future. Apart from erasing the "begging bowl" image of India, the most important gain has been the saving of forests and land, thanks to the productivity improvement associated with high yielding varieties. This year, Indian farmers harvested over 60 million tonnes of wheat, as compared to 6 million tonnes at the time of our Independence in 1947. Punjab farmers have raised the average yield of wheat to over 40 quintals per hectare. Likewise, Tamil Nadu farmers have raised the average yield of rice to over 50 quintals per hectare. If the yield improvement associated with the Green Revolution in wheat and rice had not taken place, we will need another 70 million hectares to produce the wheat and rice we now harvest. Thus, the productivity inmprovement associated with the Green Revolution is best described as forest and land saving agriculture. The productivity improvement has taken place not only in wheat and rice but also in relation to milk and eggs. Only in the case of pulses, we are lagging behind.

The population of India is growing at a rate of 1.8 per cent per year. If this trend continues, our population will double itself in less than 40 years. Only Kerala, Tamil Nadu, Goa and Mizoram have so far achieved a demographic transition to low birth and death rates. Besides population increase, improved purchasing power among the poor will enhance the demand for food, since undernutrition and poverty go together. In contrast, per capita availability of arable land is shrinking. Water efficiency is still on the whole low and water disputes are growing. In addition to the gradual decline in per capita availability of land and water, various forms of biotic and abiotic stresses are spreading. There is still a widespread mismatch between production and post-harvest technologies. In perishable commotities like fruits, vegetables, flowers, meat and other animal products, this mismatch is often severe, affecting the inyterests of both producers and consumers. This is why foreign experts frequently refer to the setting in of a fatigue of the Green Revolution. Lester Brown and Hal Kane in their book "Full House" released last year predict that at the current rate of population growth and environmental degradation coupled with an improvement in the consumption capacity of the poor, India will have to import annually over 40 million tonnes of food grains by the year 2030. This is four times the quantity we imported in 1966 i.e. before the onset of the Green Revolution. We should examine this issue seriously and should not allow complacency overtake the farm sector, just because we now have over 30 million tonnes of food grains available with Government.

Industrial countries are responsible for much of the global environmental problems such as potential changes in temperature, precipitation, sea level and incidence of ultraviolet-B radiation. While further agricultural intensification in industrialised countries will be ecologically disastrous, the failure to achieve agricultural intensification and diversification in developing countries where farming provides most of the jobs will be socially disastrous. This is because, agriculture including crop and animal husbandary, forestry and agro-forestry, fisheries and agro-industries provides livelihood to over

70 per cent of our population. The smaller the farm, the greater is the need for higher marketable surplus for increasing income. Eleven million new livelihoods will have to be created every year in India and these have to come largely from the farm and rural industries sectors. Importing food and other agricultural commodities will hence have the same impact as importing unemployment. Thus, what we need now is an environmentally sustainable and socially equitable green revolution or what may be termed as ever-green revolution.

Those who advocate going back to the old methods of farming ignore the fact that just a century ago when the population of undivided India was 281 million, famines claimed 30 million lives between 1870 and 1900. The famine eradication strategy of India comprising the following steps is perhaps the most important achievement of independent India:

- — Enhanced production and productivity.
- — Better distribution through the public distribution system.
- — Adequate grain reserves.
- — Purchasing power enhancement through various employment generation and guarantee schemes.
- — Special intervention programmes for children, pregnant and nursing mothers and old and infirm persons.

While famines have been prevented, widespread under-nutrition prevails among the economically underprivileged. Since non-food factors like health care, environmental hygiene and literacy play an important role in promoting sustainable food security of the level of the individual, we should redefine security.

Steps for achieveing sustainable food security are as under:

First sustained physical access to food will involve a transition from chemical and machnery intensive to ecological farming technologies.

Second, the emphasis on economic access underlines the need for promoting sustainable livelihoods through multiple income-earning opportunities.

Third, environmental access involves on the one hand attention to soil health care, water harvesting management and the conservation of forest and biodiversity, and on the other to sanitation, environment hygiene, primary health care and primary education.

If the political vision to implement this mission is forthcoming, population stabilisation can be more readily achieved. The prediction of Margins de Condorcet made in 1975 that population will stabilise itself, if children are born for happiness and not just for existence, will then come true.

The emphasis on the individual is important, since the household is not often a homogenous unit. Women and girl children tend to suffer more from under-nutrition than men and boys. UNDP's 1995 Human Development Report contains distressing data on the growing feminisation of poverty. To give operational content to such a concept of food security, we should initiate a Hunger-Free Area Programme (HFAP) consisting of the following components:

— Ensuring sustainable availability of food production over population growth through the development and dissemination of ecotechnologies, supported by appropriate packages of services and public policies. Ecotechnology involves the blending of the ecological prudence and technologies of the past, with the best in frontier technologies, particularly biotechnology, information technology, space technology, renewablre energy technology and management technology. Without ecotechnological empowerment, farm men and women will not be able to produce more food and other agricultural commodities on an environmentally sustainable basis from less land, water and energy resources.

— Sustain the productivity of the natural resource base, by conserving and improving the ecological foundations essential for continuous advances in crop and animal productivity.

— Ensure adequacy of household incomes through promotional social security, such as accessing assets, employment and organisational and marketing empowerment. Agricultural programmes should concurrently aim at more food, more jobs and more income. Integrated attention to farm and non-farm employment and value-addition to primary agricultural commodities will be necessary to enhance income and rural livelihood security.

— Provide entitlement to food through protective social security measures to the vulnerable groups, such as employment guarantee and food for nutrition programmes.

— Introduce a National Food and Livelihood Security Act for the purpose of paying integrated attention to:

Conservation of lands, water, forests, biodiversity and the protection of the atmosphere.

Enchancing productivity through ecotechnologies.

Improving distribution in order to eliminate endemic hunger.

Maintenance of adequate food security reserves.

Strengthneing the techno-infrastructure for better post-harvest technology and expanding the coverage of sanitary and phytosanitary measures, and

Efficient research, education, extension, marketing systems both to take full advantage of emerging opportunities in international trade and to ensure that research and extension designed to promote public good receive adequate support.

Agricultural Growth

The rate of agricultural growth of the order of around 3.2 per cent per annum during the fifties was derived from acreage increases to the extent of 70 per cent. In the sixties, the rate of growth which was only 2.1 per cent in this sector and did not neutralize even the rate of increase of population in that decade, could be derived from acreage increase to the extent of 30 per cent only. The scope for any further increase in acreage for increasing agricultural peoduction has exhausted in the seventies and the entire increase in farm production had to come from improvement in per acre productivity. This has required high level of capital–intensive effort in the development of the agricultural sector.

According to a competent study, the capital output ratio in Indian agriculture has already touched the figure of four and is close to the same scale as is required in industry. For the same reason, the fact has to be reckoned with that absorption of labour in agriculture through a significant rise in yields on land has tended to be a comparatively limited and expensive process and this process alone cannot be relied upon to solve the growing unemployment problem. The running controversy on priorities as between agriculture and industry, in particular heavy industry, is thus futile and misleading in the context of the realities of Indian economic situation and its growth prospects. The idea that India enjoys a comparative advantage in agricultural output inIndia is now crucially dependent on growth of inputs from industry.

The need is thus not to fforeclose available resources in the economy for the so called development needs of the agricultural sector but to mop up a substained part of the surpluses and incremental incomes generating in the agricultural sector to meet the investment requirements of infrastructural development, including heavy and intermediate goods industries,to inputs for agriculture at a rapid and accelerating pace.

If much credit is taken for achieving self—sufficiency in food grains relative to effective domestic demand, there is now much brave talk of making India one of the few "grain powers" in the world even while large number of Indian people still do not have access to adequate food. Agriculture in India will have to go a long way yet before it can feed the Indian people. It is too early to talk of India becoming a "grain power." But the official policy has already veered to the postion that the government would not come in the way of the farmers exporting their produce and these exports would not be banned "merely" for bringing supplies and prices down for the domestic consumers. The upshot has been that while good grains have been exported, two million tonnes of wheat are being imported in the current year, 1996—97 to meet even the effective demand in the domestic market. The danger inherent in this position is not imaginary.

The widening disparities in incomes and levels of living combined with growing concentration of land and the swelling ranks of landless rural labourers are manifest. It is not amiss either to consider the pricing of agricultural produce, more especially food grains—the primary wage goods—and examine its influence on the general price trend and structure of relative prices in the Indian economy. The Agricultural Prices Commission, to start with, recommended a particular set of prices based on its studies of the cost of production, fair return to the farmer and fair prices for the consumer.

It has been a practice, by and large, to improve upon the prices recommended by the APC in order to provide additional incentives to the surplus farmers to increase production for the market. After the launching of the so—called economic reforms in 1991, however, the baalance between the claims of the surplus farmer and the consumer has been tilting sharply in favour of the former and the inflationary impact of "incentive prices" for good grains and other agricultural produce has been ignored. Subsidised farming by way of what are called "incentive prices" for farm produce and subsidised inputs for agriculture like chemical fertilizers, private irrigation facilities like tubewells and pumpsets, power andcomparative soft—term credit, was conceived in the wake of the disastrous drought years of 1964-65 as the means of stimulating agricultural production for the market and securing control over a substantial part of the marketable surpluses so produced.

There were probably compelling reasons under the given ownership pattern in cultivable land for adopting this strategy when shortages of agricultural commodities, especially of food grains, ad emerged as an endemic problem of the economy—its stability and further growth. But the concomitant of this development has been the growing commercialization of agriculture and emergence within it to prominence of that segment of farmers with their commercial interests which produce and control agricultural surpluses. In the course of time, however, as shortage in cereals or other crops are overcome relative, of course, to effective market demand at the present low-level of purchasing power in the economy, the system of subsidised production and marketing in agriculture has become in essence a mechanism to ensure to the surplus producer a monopoly to all the gains arising from incrreases in production and productivity.

Among the vast numbers of Indian farmers, only a small fraction, and more than 10 per cent of the total, commanding the best cultivable land produces for the market on any scale. They also monopolise the subsidised supply of inputs and credit and benefits of infrastructural facilities such as irrigation and power created by public investment.

The official planners have been very brave, indeed foolhardy, to scale up from 3.5 per cent to 4.5 per cent, reportedly under political pressure, the agricultural growth rate target for the Ninth Plan. This may please the powerful lobby of rich farmers and pander to their high growth ambitions. But it casts grave doubts on the veracity and credibility of the planning exercise, especially so when the sharp set-back to agricultural production in 1995-96, a good monsoon year, should have made the planners doubly cautious in their approach to the ticklish problems and uncertain prospects of Indian agriculture.

Disturbing trends

The disturbing indications that really must hot be ignored cavalierly are that the Green Revolution in irrigated areas based on viable farmers and subsidized inputs especially chemical fertilizers, may have touched the plateau. Also to reckon with is the shrinking social base of farming, with small and marginal farmers being squeezed out and the big gentlemen farmers with large land holdings and access to modern inputs and technologies furiously developing a nexus with urban business corporations, including multinational corporations. The agricultural growth target of 4.5 per cent for the Ninth Five Year Plan may, in this context, make some sense only if it is projected not for the total production or food security for the people of India, especially half the population suffering from poverty, hunger and malnutrition, but for marketable surpluses to meet effective demand, that is demand backed by purchasing power for agricultural products, including food grains, in the domestic and the global markets.

The performance of Indian agriculture after gaining political independence has been impressive and should not be derided as has been done by the votaries of the market-oriented growth of industry as well as agriculture. Food production quadrupled between 1951 and 1991. There was also significant growth of what are known as case crops to augment supplies for a wide variety of processing industries. This success was achieved with positive intervention of the Indian State, including large public investment in irrigation, research and development and, supplies of subsidized inputs like quality seeds, fertilizers and power. This was combined with judicious support prices for agricultural produce, especially food grains. Since the launching of the so-called economic reform policies in 1991 to bring about what is loftily claimed to be the structural adjustment of the Indian economy, the position of Indian agriculture has changed ominously. The fluctuations in agriculture production have become sharper. There is shift away from food grains to cash crops. Within the food crops, production of rice and wheat has been given generous price and other incentives. The production of coarse cereals, pulses and grains has tended to decline. With the per capita availability of cereals declining, the poor have been hit hard by their rising prices. The nature and content of agricultural growth has not even been properly comprehended, let alone tackled in the approach paper on the Ninth Plan.

New strategy in the sixties

A marked feature of agricultural policy or what is known as the new agricultural strategy launched in the mid-sixties was a decisive shift of emphasis from institutional reform to technological improvement. This found expression in the organization of modern inputs for viable farming. Expansion of irrigation, especially on private account, and supply of chemical fertilizers, pesticide and quality seeds registerd a relatively big advance and helped to enhance production and productivity of farmers with addess to these facilities. Since the farmers with marketable surpluses were at the same time assured of rising levels of incentive-procurement prices, the govenment was able, side to mop up adequate qualities of agricultural produce, especially of food grains, for current consumption well as building up of the buffer stocks.

The problem of feeding the urban population and the growing non-agricultural force was acute in the fifties and the sixties. This was indeed the biggest stumbling block in the way of overall economic stability and growth. Reliance on aided imports of food grains necessarily imposed sever strains, economic and political. It may well be claimed that Indian agriculture has by now developed to a point where it is in a position to meet effective demand for food grains in the Indian market. In this sense, the agrarian crisis as it manifested itself till the mid-seventies can be said to have been resolved. But the question now to be faced is the further growth of agriculture, its content and direction.

It is not without significance either that land reforms are no longer projected in official policy as an essential prerequisite for overcoming bottlenecks to higher production and productivity in agriculture. They are at best treated as desirable purely from the social justice angle. The talk of land reforms which the political leaders indulge in from time to time is, is therefore more of a populist gesture that carries little conviction in the political power system.

The prospect of growth in agriculture in 1996-97 appears to be excellent and the year is likely to end up with foodgrains production of over 191.2 million tonnes as against 185 million tonnes in the preceding year. In commercial crops, particularly oilseeds, and cotton, significant increase in output is quite certain. The only area of concern, however, is the continued slow growth in production of pulses. Overall, the agriculture production is likely to record a growth rate of about 3 per cent in 1996-97.

1996 was the ninth successive normal monsoon year. Country wide seasonal rainfall was 103 per cent of the long—term average which was better than that of last year. The monsoon arrived almost on time and covered the entire country by June 30, two weeks earlier than the normal date. By the end of the Monsoon season (June-September),32 out of 35 meterological sub-division and 81 per cent of districts covering 91 per cent area of the country had received normal to excess rainfall. The comparative performance of the monsoon for the past ten years, 1987 to 1996. The district-wise distribution of rainfall for the past 10 years.

The spatial and temporal rainfall distribution over the country was very satisfactory except over Orrissa and Vidarbha where rainfall was marginally deficient or scanty in some districts. In the later part of June,

Rajasthan and Haryana experienced floods. In third week of July, floods also occured in north Bengal and Bihar. Excessive rain due to cyclonic storm caused extensive damage twice in Andhra Pradesh, first in June and then again in early November.

Total rainfall, its spatial and temporal distribution and its impact on the production of Kharif cereals, can be seen from the rice area and production weighted rainfall index constructed for each State and aggregated over All India. Cereals production weighted cumulative rainfall indices for the entire season are computed by assigning weights based on share in the production of kharif cereals. A comparative picture of temporal distribution of rainfall during the sout-west monsoon season of 1996 as compared to 1995 and 1994.

Rabi prospects also depend to some extent on post monsoon rainfall. The cumulative rainfall during the post sout-west monsoon season 1996 (1 October to 31 December) was excess or normal in 25 meteorological sub-divisions as against 16 subdivisions during the corresponding period last year. Performance of the post-monsoon rainfall for the past 6 years.

The main states or division which received deficient or scanty rainfall during the post monsoon period are Gangetic West Bengal, Sub-Himalayan West Bengal and Sikkim, Orissa, Bihar Plateau, Jammu & Kashmir, Himachal Pradesh, Punjab, Haryana, Chandigarh, Delhi, Hills of West Uttar Pradesh and East Madhya Pradesh.

The total live storage position in 63 important reservoirs in different part of the country by the end of September, 1996 as monitored by the Central Water Commission was much better this year. It was 97.7 Thousand Million Cubic Meters (TMC) at the end of September, 1996 as against 90.1 TMC during the corresponding period of 1995. Comperative position of storage level at the end of September, 1996. Agriculture production performance in the last five years together with the prospects for 1996-97.

Foodgrains account for about 63 per cent of country's agricultural output and hence even a marginal decline in foodgrains production has a 'ripple effect' on rest of the economy. Despite a near normal monsoon in 1995, the foodgrains output of 185 million tonnes in 1995-96 was lower by over 6 million tonnes. This was mainly on account of decrease in production of wheat, kharif rice, bajra and pulses. The most unexpected development was the late realisation in 1996 that the wheat harvest was just about 62.6 million tonnes, lower by about 3 million tonnes over the preceding year. The reasons for decline in production of rabi foodgrain crops i.e. wheat conditions at the grain filling stage of the crop in February/March, 1996. This was a serious set back and its late realisation did cause some distortions in wheat availability. Wheat prices rose to unprecedented heights by November, 1996, promoting the Government to release larger quantities from FCI's public stocks besides taking recourse to imports. Kharif 1996 foodgrains output is likely to be 103.2 million tonnes as against only 98.2 million tonnes in 1995. If Rabi crops prospects turn out to be normal, 1996-97 foodgrains output is likely to be 191.2 million tonnes which would be close to the record production of 191.5 million tonnes achieved in 1994-95. The annual growth rate in foodgrain production in recent past.

Per hectare yield rates of rice and wheat rose significantly during seventies and eighties. Consequently, both these foodgrains registered over 3 over per cent annual growth in production between 1980-81 to 1995-96, which was significantly higher than the annual population growth of 2.14 per cent during eighties. The low annual growth of 1.2 per cent in production of pulses since 1980-81 did, however, looking at the first seven years of this decade (1990-91 to 1996-97), the annual rate of growth of foodgrains was only 1.7 per cent which is lower than the current population growth. If this trend continues it could become a matter of grave concern.

Rice production reached a record level of 81.8 million tonnes in 1995 However, production in 1995-96 was down to 79.6 million tonnes. Production in Kharif, 1996 is estimated to be 70.6 million tonnes compared to 70.1 million tonnes in Kharif, 1995. Some adverse impact on rabi/summer rice during 1996-97 on account of the deficient/scanty rains, particularly in Orissa and West Bengal and also on account of cyclonic strom in Andhra Pradesh, has been reported. Despite this, if 1996 Rabi rice output remains at 1994-95 or 1995 or 1995-96 level of around 9 million tonnes, the total output of rice may be 79.6 million tonnes in 1996-97.

Wheat output of 62.6 million tonnes in 1995-96 was 3.2 million tonnes lower over 1994-95 output of 65.8 million tonnes. Due to sudden rise in temperature at the grain filling stage of the crop in February/March, 1996, there was an unexpected decline in its productivity in major wheat growing States except Haryana and Rajasthan. Service incidence of yellow rust was also reported on wheat variety HD-2329 which is largely grown in Punjab. 1996-97 target of wheat output is 65 million tonnes. The weather parameter of temperature was initially low, which is considered beneficial for the crop growth. However, delayed winter rains in the wheat growing area have resulted in moisture stress conditions. If the rainfall/temperature conditions are normal in the Rabi season, the production of wheat may be relatively better and could be expected at around 64.50 million tonnes in 1996-97. Wheat is becoming important even in rice consuming areas and increasingly subsituting for coarse cereals as urbanisation and incomes rise. The ratio of wheat production to rice production has steadily increased from one third in 1950-51 and 1960-61 to about one half in 1970-71 and further to four fifth in 1995-96.

The area under coarse grains (bajra, maize, jowar, ragi, small millets and barley) continues to show a declining trend and stagnation in production. Coarse grains are mostly grown by small and marginal farmers in areas largely characterised by low and erratic rainfall. The coarse grains are grown mostly in Maharashtra, Rajasthan, Madhya Pradesh, Uttar Pradesh, Andhra Pradesh, Tamil Nadu and Bihar. In 1995-96, the production of all the coarse cereal crops except bajra was relatively better than 1994-95. The production of bajra in 1995-96 suffered badly in the major States of Rajashtan, Gujarat, Haryana and Maharashtra and was 5.39 million tonnes i.e. substantially lower by 24.7 per cent over the production level of 7.16 million tonnes achieved in 1994-95. Despite this, the production of coarse cereals is estimated to be 29.1 million tonnes in 1995-96. As the rainfall and weather situation, particularly during the monsoon period, has been quite favorable in the major coarse cereal growing States, the production prospects have improved and the coarse cereal out is expected to be about 33.05 million tonnes in 1996-97.

Pulses production in the country has been stagnating around 8-14 million tonnes for the last 40 years. Per capital availability of pulses has come down from 69 grams in 1961 to about 39 grams in 1996. Production fluctuates from year to year depending on the performance of monsoon. The practice of inter cropping and mixed cropping is also more prevalent in pulses, which are grown as secondary crops. The production of pulses, which crossed 14 million tonnes in 1995-96. This was due to the substantial fall in production of gram to

5.02 million tonnes in 1995-96 from a level of 6.44 million tonnes in the preceding year. This shortfall was, however, offset to some extent by higher production achieved in Tur and other pulses in 1995-96. As a result of better monsoon rainfall, the production of pulses is expected to be higher and may be around 14 million tonnes in 1996-97.

The production of commercial crops like sugarcane (283 million tonnes), oilseeds (22.4 million tonnes) cotton (13.1 million bales) have been of a record level in 1995-96. As per the present assessment, the production prospects of these crops are better in 1996-97 and the production may go up further.

Sugarcan production reached a record level of 275.54 million tonnes in 1994-95 surpassing its earlier record level of 254 million tonnes of 1991-92. Again, a record production of 283 million tonnes of sugarcane has been estimated for 1995-96. Current production prospects of sugarcane are also quite good and is expected to be about 274 million tonnes in 1996-97.

Sugar production reached an all time record level of about 164 lakh tonnes in sugar year 1995-96 (October, 1995 to September, 1996), recording a substantial jump over the precedng years of record production of 146 lakh tonnes. Two years of record output of sugar has resulted in accumulation of sizable stocks, and industry is striving to export more, depending upon whether the global prices are favorable. The Statutory Minimum Price (SMP) for sugarcane for 1995-96 was fixed at Rs. 42.50 per quintal linked to a basic recovery of 8.5 per cent and for the 1996-97 season it has been fixed at Rs. 45.90 per quintal.

The sugar industry continues to function under a regulatory system where licences have to be sought for establishing new capacity or expanding the existing installed capacity. There is also a dual price control system under which 40 per cent of output is pre-empted for use of the government for PDS, at an ex-factory price which is fixed for each of 16 Zones. The balance 60 per cent output, factories are free to sell at the market price except that the quantity for free saie is regaulated by precscribing monthly quantities that each units can sell as non-levy sugar.

During the financial year 1995-96, the releases for PDS ranged from 3.27 to 4.03 lakh tonnes per month. Similarly, the releases for freesale sugar were kept high between 6.25 to 8.30 lakh MTs per month so as to ensure that freesale market price of sugar remained at a reasonable level. The stock holding limits and turnover period of sugar and khandasari were enhanced to 1000 quintals and 30 days from 1st October, 1996 from 500 quintals and 15 days respectively to promote increased availability of sugar in the market.

During the 1995-96 sugar season, about 8.87 lakh tonnes of sugar was exported. Sugar export has been decanalized and manufacturing units are now permitted to pack sugar in 50 kg. packages for export purposes and from 5th November, 1996, also in small consumer packs of 1, 2 and 5 kgs. for indigenous use. These packages can be made from any foodgrade packaging material.

Among the nine oilseed crop grown in the country, groundnut and rapeseed/mustard together for 62 per cent of total oilseeds production. Soyabean and sunflower have to late emerged as the oilseed crops having major growth potential. The other oilseed crops include seasamum, castorseed, nigerseed, safflower linseed. Oilseeds production was 18.61 million tonnes in 1990-91 and has since touched a level of 22.42 million tonnes in 1995-96. The production in 1996-97 is likely to be 24.11 million tonnes.

Cotton production is estimated at 130.9 lakh bales of 170 kgs. each in 1995-96, and increase of 10.1 per cent over the production of 118.9 lakh bales in 1994-95. Due to increase both in area coverage and its productivity, the production of cotton is likely to go up further in 1996-97 an is expected to be around 143 lakh bales.

Production of Jute and Mesta continued to stagnate. Production which had reached a record level during 1995-86, registered a sharp decline and hovered around 6.78 to 10.29 million bales thereafter. Production in 1995-96 is expected to be 8.90 million bales, and may rise marginally to 9.19 million bales in 1996-97.

Crop production

Agricultural crop production in 1996—97 is expected to show good recovery from the slower growth in 1995—96. Growth is projected at 3 per cent after a fall of 0.4 per cent in 1995—96. The sharp decline in foodgrains production by 3.4 per cent, which was responsible for the slow growth in 1995—96, is expected to be reversed by an increased of 3.3 per cent in 1996—97. Foodgrains production is expected to recovery is primarily due to coarse cereals, as well as an anticipated rise in wheat production which suffered a sharp setback in 1995—96.

As the agricultureal year runs from July to June, the estimates for 1995—96 were only firmed up after the end of the financial year. A large downward revision (of 3 million tonnes) was made in the estimate of wheat production for 1995—96. The revision was unexpected and unexplained, because average rainfall in 1995—96 was quite normal. The revision, late in calendar year 1996, also created severe problems for the management of the food economy.

Commercial crop production has done extremely well in 1996—97 with oilseeds and cotton expected to reach record levels of 24.1 million tonnes and 14.3 million tonnes, respectively. Jute and mesta have also shown a growth of 3.4 per cent this year. Sugarcane output is, however, unlikely to maintain the record level of 283 million tonnes attained in 1995—96.

Industrial production (as measured by the index of industrial production–IIP), grew by 9.8 per cent in the first seven months of 1996—97, 1.9 percentage points slower than the 11.7 per cent growth in the in the corresponding period of 1995—96. The good performance of industrial production in 1996—97 is due entirely to the manufacturing sector, which has maintained its high growth.

The slowing of industrial production is clearly attributable to the dramatic fall in the rate of growth of electricity production and a slowing of growth in the mining sector mainly because of the 10 per cent decline in crude oil production. During the first seven months of 1996—97, electricity production (as measured by the index) has grown by only 3.4 per cent compared to the 10.1 per cent growth in the corresponding period of 1995—96. It is somewhat surprising that manufacturing sector growth has been barely affected by the slow growth in electricity production. One possibility is that captive electricity generation, which is increasingly used as a back—up to public supply, has substituted for the lack of generation by electricity boards. The high growth of diesel imports, about 22 per cent by volume in the first seven months of 1996—97 (with total refinery throughput growing in the normal range of around 4 per cent), is consistent with this hypothesis. At present, electricity statistics incorporate little or no data on captive power generation.

Another noteworthy aspect of industrial growth this year is the acceleration in the rate of growth of capital goods production to 16.6 per cent in the first seven months of this year from 15 per cent in the first seven months of last year. This has off—set the decline in the rate of growth of consumer goods and basic goos. In contrast, capital goods imports have declined by 6 per cent in the first seven months of 1996—97. This shows the increased competitiveness of the domestic capital goods industry. The overall performance of the core and infrastructure sectors during the first 8 months of 1996—97 (April—November) has been poor.

Six industries namely, electricity generation, coal, steel, crude oil, petroleum products and cement, with a combined weight of 28.8 per cent in the Index of Industrial Production (IIP), averaged a growth of 4.1 per cent in April—November, 1996, less than half the 8.9 per cent, in April—November, 1995. The deceleration in the growth rate of these infrastructure industries is mainly due to a decline in crude oil production and power generation. Hydro power generation declined by 7.7 per cent, and thermal power generation grew by only 6.4 per cent in the April—November, 1996 as compared to 14.6 per cent in the April—March, 1995—96. Coal, cement and refineries' throughput have grown faster in April—November, 1996—97 compared to the corresponding period of 1995—96. Growth of sectors such as railways, ports and telecommunications, which do not appear in the IIP, also slowed. The rate of growth of railways' revenue earning goods traffic decelerated marginally from 7 per cent during 1995—96 to 6.3 per cent for April–November 1996. Growth of cargo handled at major ports and new telephone connections provided decelerated more sharply to 4.7 per cent in April—November, 1996 (from 9.1 per cent in 1995—96) and 8.3 per cent in April—November, 1996 (from 23.3 per cent in 1995–96), respectively. The slower growth in cargo handled by ports in probably the result of a deceleration in the growth of external trade. The telecomunications slowdown, however, suggests that the pace of implementation of telecommunications reform needs to be accelerated and its scope widened to include Department of Telecommunications as a service provider. Given the parlous financial state of many public utilities, particularly the State Electricity Boards, the possibility of crises worsens with each passing year. The new government has repeatedly stressed its firm determination to reform the infrastructure and energy sectors. In line with this commitment, a number of policy decisions have been taken and new initiatives launched.

The second International Crop Science Congress, held in New Delhi from November 17 to 24, has displayed the International scientific community's will to solve the mankind's basic problem of hunger and to lay the foundation for a vibrant, yet ecologically sustainable, agriculture to meet future needs. The world's largest assembly of crop scientists, over 1500 from nearly 70 countries, emphasised that the modern biotechnology, coupled with traditional wisdom, can mould future to suit the interest of the human society. Though new challenges will keep cropping up, the science would perhaps not only be able to deal with them but might indeed convert them into opportunities for the good of humanity.

The optimism would, however, hold true only if it is matched by political will to raise farm productivity as also to distribute its gains equitably. New technology accompanied by appropriate marketing policies and international cooperation holds the key to ensuring foods security in the years to come.

Deliberations of the mega scientific event, organised jointly by the National Academy of Agricultural Sciences (NAAS) and the Indian Council of Agricultural research

(ICAR), once again confirmed the widely held notion that while the scientists would be able to cope with humanity's needs they may become helpless to cope with its greed. The world renowned agricultural expert, Dr. M.S. Swaminathan, who chaired the Congress, did not mince words in passing on this message. He said: "Whether in agriculture or aquaculture, we must curb the greed revolution and promote an ever-green revolution capable of bringing about continuous advances in terrestrial and aquatic productivity without harm to the environmental capital stocks of land, water forests, biological diversity, oceans and climate upon which such advances depend."

The theme of the Congress, "Crop productivity and sustainability—shaping the future"—was highly appropriate and topical for several reasons. Despite phenomenal growth in food production, nearly one-fifth of the world population is still malnourished and hungry. The impact of the green revolution is waning and concerns of productivity decline in major crop production systems are being expressed globally, diminishing per capita availability of land and water resources, expanding biotic and abiotic stresses and natural resources, including land, forest and environment, are fast degrading. This calls for greater resolve to ensure synergism among productivity, profitability and sustainability of major cropping systems. Moreover, for safeguarding food and nutritional security at the household level, crop intensification and diversification are needed on an ecologically sustainable basis.

Let us now concentrate on another important aspect, e.g. the impact of Operation Barja on production. During 1972—73 to 1978—80 the foodgrain production in West Bengal grew at a rate of 1.7% as against 2.5% for India as a whole. During the decade of eighties, i.e. the post operation Barga period, the growth of food grain production in West Bengal was 3% as against India's 2.4% (Sengupta 1993). During this period West Bengal has also seen an increase in oilseeds and potato production. Although a large part of this increase may be the field of agriculture, the role of land reform in boosting agriculture cannot be totally denied. There are studies which show that the productivity of share cropped land is higher for recorded than for unrecorded share croppers (Chandra 1993).

A micro level survey conducted by Chaudhuri and Pal (1993) reveals that the productivity of self cultivated owned land is higher than that of land under share cropping arrangement (both recorded and unrecorded). The study also reveals that the use of input e.g. chemical fertilizers and high yielding variety (HYV) of seeds ar also lower in tenant operated plots. One possible reason is the poverty of the tenants which makes them incapable of purchasing fertilizer and necessary irrigation water for cultivation of HYV crops. Moreover there may be reluctance on the part of the share—croppers to invest more on a leased in plot whose output will have to be shared with the owner.

So far as the distribution of vested land is concerned, West Bengal has performed very well. At the end of 1991, 0.37 million hectares of land were distributed among 2.0 million families. In West Bengal, the two schemes, i.e. the distribution of surplus land and recording of Barga cover nearly 40% of the rural households. Most of the holdings are rainfed and hence it is not possible to raise Rabi or Boro crops on the plot. The scarcity of irrigation water affects the recorded share croppers equally. Another important problem of the owners of vested land is the scarcity of bullock power to till land. These people have to hire bullock and carts from their landlords and this may, in some cases, lead to exploitation by landlords.

The problems discussed so far may be eased by establishing cooperatives for agricultural inputs specially irrigation and bullock power. One obstacle to the formation of such cooperatives is fragmentation of land. The consolidation of holdings has not been done in most of the states.

At present the owners of adjacent holding may form groups for investing in shallow tubewells, pumpsets, bullocks and carts. In order to utilize a pair of bullocks an average of 4 to 5 acres of land is required. So formation of cooperatives is the easiest way of utilising the bullock power most economically. Tractors may also b purchased and maintained on a cooperative basis. For the success of cooperative movement special attention should be given to the consollidation of fragmented holdings.

The owners of marginal plots and also the poor share croppers should be trained properly to start various off—farm activity, e.g. cottage industries, animal husbandary, pisciculture etc. These off—farm activities will be their secondary sources of income. Loans and subsidies should also be made available to this group for starting such off—farm activities. All these will go a long way to make the land reform measures a success.

Food consumption

Against the per capita net availability of 501.9 gms of cereals the estimated consumption of cereals was of the order of 394 gms i.e. 78.6 per cent of the net availability. similarly in the case of pulses, per capita consumption was 28.05 gms. i.e. 75.8 per cent of net availability. Inequality in the consumption of foods among different income groups gets masked in the overall consumption estimates. Among the poor, nearly 80 per cent of consumption expenditure goes for food items. Recent surveys indicate:

— Percapita cereal consumption has declined over the years resulting in the aggregate energy intake of 1859 k.cal per capita as against 2200 k.cal recommended.

— 47.7 per cent of households have calorie inadequacy and 19.8 per cent of households have protein inadequacy. 19.5 per cent of households have both calorie and protein inadequacy.

— The exetent of moderate and severe growth retardation in preschool children varied from 34 per cent in Kerala to 72 per cent in Gujarat.

— 47 per cent of adults have body mass index value below 18.5 indicating large scale prevalance of chronic energy deficiency in the community.

— Haemoglobin levels among pregnant mothers reveal that as many as 87.5 per cent of mothers were anaemic.

— About 30 per cent of infants born had low birth weight.

— 167 million people are considered to be at risk for iodine deficiency disorders and 54 million have goitre.

— Preventable blindness due to Vitamin A deficiency still large.

Looking back the distance travelled and counting on various milestones towards food security, the country can be proud of some of the achievements so far. Yet the final milestone looks to be a long march. Shrinking arable land resources, soil degradation and depletion of nutrients from the soil, poor water management and unsustainable use of ground water, loss of momentum in the growth of food output, inefficient biological utilisation of the nutrients consumed due to poor environment and growing population are some of the problems the country faces in the march towards the final milestone of a hunger-free nation. The over-exploitation of the aquifer is also leading to the leaching of high levels of arsenic from natural underground sources into thousands of village wells in West Bengal. As estimated 200,000 people already have arsenic-induced skin lesions. It is estimated that there are about 20 million species of poants, out of which 50,000 are edible. However, we are not using more than 200 plants as food, 80 per cent of our food supply however comes only from about eight species. We are today laying much emphgasis on developing new varieties of these few plants. We should enlarge the food basket by including the excluded. Many nutritious grains fall under the classification "coarse grains". It is time we start referring to them as "nutritious grains". They are rich in micronutrients like Fe and Ca.

The momentum of growth witnessed in 1995—96 with a GDP growth of over 7 per cent, has been maintained in 1996—97, thus providing increasing evidence that the growth potential has improved as a result of the reforms initiated in 1991. With the growing participation of virtually the entire spectrum of political opinion inthe reform process, there is a good prospect that a higher growth rate would become a permanent feature of the economy.

The initial spurt of reforms from 1991—92 to 1993—94 was very successful by all accounts, resulting in a jump in economic growth to 7.2 per cent in 1994—95 (in terms of GDP at factor cost). Since 1994—95, however, there was a marked slow down in the pace of reforms. Nevertheless, GDP grew by 7.1 per cent in 1995—96. The slackening of reforms preceding and during the election period may have been responsible for some loss of momentum, but this has been revived with a series of measures in recent months.

Economic growth in 1996—97 is estimated by CSO to be around 6.8 per cent (GDP at factor cost). Thus, the Eighth Plan is likely to end with an average growth of 6.5 per cent per annum, 0.9 per cent point higher than the target rate of 5.6 per cent, and 0.5 per cent point higher than the actual achievement of the Seventh Plan. More important for the future is the fact that the average growth during the latest three years is 7 per cent, probably placing India among the top ten performers in the world during this period.

As the final year of the Eighth Plan draws to a close, a comparison of some salient dimensions of some salilent dimensions of economic performance between the Eighth Plan period and its predecessor reveals the following:

— Overall economic growth has been faster;

— The manufacturing sector has grown almost 2 per cent points faster per year in the Eighth Plan period;

— Agriculture and allied sectors have grown at about 3.5 per cent per annum in both periods;

— Both exports and imports have grown significantly faster in the Eighth Plan period;

— The balance of payments has strengthened considerably, with trade and current account deficits declining as ratios of GDP; while exports and imports have grown rapidly both in value terms as well as in proportion to GDP.

— The Central Government's fiscal deficit as a proportion of GDP has declined significantly;

— The average rate of gross domestic savings has risen substantially from 20.6 per cent of GDP in the Seventh Plan period to 23.9 per cent in the first four years of the Eighth Plan;

— With the exception of telecommunications, the rate of growth of net output (value added) of infrastructure sectors has slowed;

— The average rate of inflation has risen somewhat, though remaining below double digits.

Total gross domestic saving reached a new peak of 25.6 per cent of GDP in 1995—96, exceeding its previous peak of 24.9 per cent of GDP in 1994–95. This seems to vindicate the reform strategy of encouraging savings by expanding saving and investment opportunities, rather than giving special incentives.

Gross domestic investment (adjusted), as a proportion of GDP at current prices, rose even faster than gross domestic saving in 1995—96 to a high of 27.4 per cent from 26 per cent in the previous year. Gross domestic investment in real terms, as a proportion of GDP at constant prices, reached a new peak of 27.1 per cent, exceeding the previous peak of 25.9 per cent in 1990—91. Gross fixed capital formation which is even more important for productivity and growth, reached a new peak of 24.1 per cent of GDP in 1995—96. Private sector investment appears to have responded vigorously to the policy of promoting competition, removing policy distortions and hurdles, and improving access to factors of production (e.g. technology, capital).

Estimates of savings and investment in 1996—97 are not yet available. Indicators are mixed. On the one hand, domestic capital goods production is buoyent and disbursement of financial institutions are significantly higher, on the other hand, capital goods imports have declined, non—oil imports are lower in the first nine months of the year, corporate demand for credit appears slack, and sanctions of financial institutions are substantially lower.

The economy in 1996—97 so far presents a mixed picture in other dimensions as well. Although overall economic growth remains high at 6.8 per cent, and agriculture has rebounded, the growth of manufacturing value added has slowed and the performance of key infrastructure sectors, especially power and crude oil, is weak. The annual rate of inflation (point to point) has risen back to average long—term levels and export growth has decelerated markedly in recent months. Despite the slowdown in exports, a combination of sluggish imports and reasonably buoyant inflows of invisibles and capital flows have led to a build—up of foreign exchange reserves by over $ 2.5 billion.

Agriculture and Indian economy

The Economic Survey–1996—97 is a balanced appraisal of the past performance of the economy, attributing the gains to the policy of economic reform and liberalisaton, pursued during the last five years and presents a picture of cautious optimism for the future. While attributing the past gains to the policy of liberalisation, the Survey asserts that the policy would need to be pursued with greater vigour in future to carry the economy to higher growth path. It attributes "the loss of momentum" in the economy to "the marked slow down in the pace of reforms preceding and during the election period", but adds "this has been revived with a series of measures in recent months."

The Survey says "the initial spurt of reforms from 1991—92 t 1993—94 was very successful on all accounts, resulting in a jump in economic growth in 1994—95 to

7.2 per cent." It says GDP grew by 7.1 per cent in 1995—96 despite the slowdown in the momentum of reform and adds, econmic growth in 1996—97 is estimated by the CSO to be around 6.8 per cent (GDP at factor cost). The Eight Plan, it says is thus likely to end with an average growth of 6.5 per cent per annum, 0.9 per cent higher than the target rate of 5.6 per cent and 0.5 per cent point higher than the actual achievement of the Seventh Plan. More important for the future is the fact that the average growth during the latest three years is 7 per cent, probably placing India among the top ten performers in the world during the period." However, when it comes to a review of sectoral performance that he Survey is compelled to be more realistic. It says "the economy in 1996–97 so far presents a mixed picture." Although, it says "overall economic growth remains high at 6.8 per cent, and agriculture has rebounded, the growth of manufacturing value added has slowed and the performance of key infrastructure sectors, especially power and crude oil, is weak. The annual rate of inflation (point to point) has risen t actual long—term levels and export growth has decelerated markedly in recent months."

On agriculture, the Survey says "production in 1996—97 is expected to show good recovery from the slower growth in 1995—96. The growth is projected at 3 per cent after a fall of 0.4 per cent in 1995–96. The sharp decline in foodgrains production by 3.4 per cent, which was responsible for the slow growth in 1995–96, is expected to be reversed by; an increase of 3.3 per cent in 1996—97. Foodgrains production is expected to recover to 191.2 million tonnes, only marginally lower than the level of production in 1994—95. The recovery is primarily due to coarse cereals, as well as anticipated rise in wheat production, which suffered a sharp setback in 1995—96." Commercial crop production has done extremely well in

1996—97 with oilseeds and cotton expected to reach record levels of 24.1 and 14.1 million tonnes respectively.

In the previous chapter, we described the situation as it prevailed in 1960-61. We shall now proceed to take a brief review of the progress made during the past decade. The last year for which some data are available is 1968-69. Therefore, in the following review, we shall cover the period from 1960-61 to 1968-69.

National Income again offers a useful summary measure to judge the performance of the economy in a given period. The particular measure of national income we shall use is specifically termed Net National Product at Factor Cost. We shall briefly refer to it as NNP. We have earlier mentioned that the NNP was Rs. 13,308 crores in 1960-61. It increased to Rs. 28,800 crores in 1968-69 was 216.4. The NNP increased annually by about 6 percentage points during 1961-62 and 1962-63; by almost 17 percentage points in 1963-64; by 26 percentage points in the next two years; by 23 percentage points in 1966-67; by 32 percentage points in 1967-68; and finally, by 6 percentage points in 1968-69. Over the eight years from 1960-61 to 1968-69, the NNP more than doubled.

This is a spectacular performance if it were all real. Unfortunately it is not all real. During the eight years from 1960-61 to 1968-69, the prices of commodities have almost doubled. This means that a rupee in 1968-69 does not mean the same thing as it did in 1960-61. Hence, to judge the real increase in NNP, we should ask what would the NNP be if the prices had remained unchanged. In other words, we should value the NNP in subsequent years at prices as they prevailed in 1960-61. We shall refer to this as Net National Product at Constant (1960-61) Prices. From such a series, it becomes clear that the NNP increased by only 26.5 per cent in eight years and not by 116.4 per cnet as appeared earlier. Thus the real increase in the NNP is only 26.5 per cent in eight years; the balance of apparent increase is a reflection of the increase in prices.

The growth in the NNP has not been steady. This is because agricultural production, which constitutes almost half of the total, is still liable to wide fluctuations from year to year. The real increase in the NNP by 6 percentage points in 1963-64 and again by 8 percentage points in 1964-65 was because of the good agricultural season in those two years. This was followed by two very bad years and the NNP actually declined in 1965-66 and remained at the same low level in 1966-67. Fortunately, the year 1967-68 turned out to be a very good year and the NNP jumped by 10 percentage points. The year 1968-69 was also a good year and the NNP is estimated to have advanced by another 2 percentage points.

Thus the anunal fluctuations in agricultural production explain the unsteady growth of the NNP. But in a period as long as 8 to 10 years, one must take good years along with bad years and reckon the fact that the real increase in NNP in eight years was only 26.5 per cent which is a compound growth rate of less than 3 per cent per annum.

The growth in the NNP must be placed alongside the growth in population. The population of the Indian Union in 1961 was 434 million. We shall know what it is when the census is taken this year. However, in the meanwhile, the population is estimated to have been growing at the annual rate of 2.5 per cent. Clearly, therefore, a growth of NNP at an annual rate of no more than 3 per cent is barely sufficient to keep pace with the growth in population; it leaves little margin to make a net improvement in the economic condition of the people. This becomes clear if we divide the NNP by the estimated population each year to get the NNP per capita. If this is done, it becomes clear that the per capita NNP increased from Rs. 306.7 in 1960-61 to just Rs. 321.3 in 1967-68 and Rs. 319.4 in 1968-69. This is an increase at best of only 4.5 per cent in eight years which is about half a per cent per annum. This summarises the performance of the economy during the past decade.

As mentioned earlier, per capita private consumer expenditure gives a more direct measure of the well-being or standard of living of a people. We have seen that the per capita private consumer expenditure was Rs. 276.3 in 1960-61. In are given the relevant data for the subsequent years. In order to assess the real changes in the per capita consumer expenditure in subsequent years at constant (1960-61) prices for the years from 1960-61 to 1968-69.

It will be seen that the per capita consumer expenditure increased from Rs. 276.3 in 1960-61 to Rs. 285.5 (at 1960-61 prices) in 1968-69. The per capita consumer expenditure shows a sudden increase (Rs. 296.0) in 1964-65 and then a sudden fall (Rs. 269.8 and Rs. 271.8) in the following two years. This is a reflection of the bumper agricultural production in 1964-65 and poor production in the following two years. The average per capita consumption during the three years 1964-65, 1965-66 and 1966-67 was Rs. 279.2 per annum. It seems more likely that the real consumption was maintained more or less at this level by carrying some of the large stocks of 1964-65 into the next two years rather than allowing it to fluctuate along with fluctuations in agricultural production. For the same reason, we should smoothen out the fluctuations in the first three years as also in the last two years. When this is done, the estimates of per capita consumer expenditure in the nine years appear as shown in. They seem more reasonable and plausible.

The upshot of the whole exercise is that the per

capita consumer expenditure rose from Rs. 276.3 in 1960-61 to Rs. 289.6 in 1968-69, that is by 4.8 per cent in eight years or by about half a per cent per annum. It is obvious that it could not have risen by any more because, we have seen as the per capita income rose at best by 4.5 per cent in the eight years.

Incidentally, we may note that the per capita consumer expenditure seems to have increased a little more than has the per capita national income. The reasons seem to be firstly that the large increase in national income registered in the last two years has been mainly on account of the large increase in the production of foodgrains in these years and secondly that the net domestic capital formation as a proportion of the net domestic expenditure has gone down sharply in these two years.

This brings us to the next point namely how are these small gains of development distributed between different sections of the population–between the rural and urban populations and between the richer and poorer sections of these populations? More specifically, we ask: The average consumer expenditure in the country rose by 4.8 per cent in real terms (that is at constant prices) in the eight years from 1960-61 and 1968-69. Did this happen equally in the case of the rural and urban populations and equally in the case of the richer and poorer sections of these populations? These questions are crucial while assessing whether anything is happening to the poor of this country; whether their lot has improved materially as a result of the economic development of the past decade. If the per capita consumption in the country has risen by no more than 4.8 per cent in eight years, it is obvious that little noticeable could have happened in the nature of alleviation of poverty unless the poorer sections have profited proportionately more than the average and much more so than the rich. Did this happen during the past decade? We shall examine the facts.

Need for strategic planning

The Ninth Five Year (1997–2002) envisages targeted food production of 230 million tonnes as against 190 million tonnes during 19945—96. Food production and its availability to at least those 39 per cent of the population living below the poverty line and around more than half (53%) of all children under the age of four, who are underweight or stunted is most essential in the context of the present socio—economic—politico environment in India.

Despite the fact that the yield of wheat and rice per hectare has appreciably increased during the post—Green Revolution period, our yields are comparatively very low. Wheat yield in India is 2,420 kg per hecatare as against 8,771 kg in the Netherlands with 2,501 kg being the Asian average. Similarly, rice yield is 2,800 kg as compared to 8,000 kg in Greece and 3,731 kg in Asia. It is also a matter of concern that India ranks 96th and 61st in the productivity of wheat and rice respectively. Irrigated land of 48 million hectares produces about 2,500 kg of food grains per hectare and rainfed area of 92 million hectares produces only about one tonne per hectare. Apart from this, wheat productivity in Punjab with 96 per cent area under irrigation is above four tonnes per hectare while it is only 2,400 kg in Uttar Pradesh with 90 per cent of irrigated wheat and only, 1,700 kg in Bihar with 86 per cent area under irrigated wheat.

In respect of rice, the annual compounded growth rat of rice yield declined considerably from 4 per cent during 1982—93 to 1.73 per cent during 1991—95 in northern zone, from 3.80 per cent to 2.62 per cent in southern zone and from 5.60 per cent to 2.08 pe cent in eastern zone as against a phenomental rise from 1.80 per cent to 5.36 per cent in western zone. Even after the advent of high yield technology, a sizeable area falls under the category oflow productivity. About 60 per cent of low productivity area are in Bihar, Orissa, Assam, West Bengal and Uttar Pradesh. It is a matter of serious concern that 32 per cent of the irrigated area are of low productivity. Studies reveal that about 30 per cent to 40 per cent of the potential yield are yet to be harvested in the available high yielding varieties in the high productivity irrigated area itself.

With the Ninth Five Year Plan (1997-2002), the Indian economy enters the 21st century and the this millennium, from which the formidable challenges facing the Plan can be guessed at. The Plan should be a turning point of the economy. In the first instance, it is good that notwithstanding a plethora of uncertainties facing the polity and the economy, the Plan could roll off setting to itself quite formidable tasks of a new century. And it augurs well for the Plan that it could muster a broad national consensus, over its approach and framework. The Plan is most likely to cheer all sections of the population with its massive investment and higher targets. Think big and act big, it seems, is the central message of the Plan, and it is incumbent on all to make a success of the Ninth Plan.

For, it must be said to the credit of Indian planning, quite an impressive one in the record of economic development and the annals of planning, that it could take the Indian economy from a small Rs. 10,000 crore GNP one to Rs. 1.2 m crore one in a span of some 45 years against all odds. What a country of diversities, pulls and pressures, size, populace, ideologies, interests, groups, divisions, threats, rebellions, riots, languor, storms and tempests! Yet, the caravan of planning moves on, pushing aside the forces of anti-development and democracy such as the zamindars and managing agents of the yester-years, to take the economy to the top brackets of the world economies, and in the process the Ninth Plan appears to be a great leap forward. It should set the trend for future unfailing planning of the country that goes a long way in alleviating the myriad economic problems facing the one billion strong Indian population growing at a Malthusian rate.

The Plan should draw lessons from the pitfalls of the previous plans and should establish proper input-output correlation and synergy. The expectations of the people are raised and they look forward to the Plan with many hopes and aspirations, particularly the common people or the masses. Marketism, to put things in proper perspective, need not come in the way of planning, as both can go hand-in-hand for common weal.. There in, so to say, nothing antagonistic between planning free enterprise.

Thus, with the decks cleared for the Ninth Plan, one may go about how it represents a new age spirit. It must be reflective of its times and must imbibe the spirit of the age, without which it cannot withstand its many challenges and steer the economy to greater heights and more satisfaction.

According to Prof Madhu Dandavate, Deputy Chairman of the Planning Commission, the Ninth Plan accords "the highest priority to generating adequate productive employment, eradication of poverty, focus on agriculture and rural development with emphasis on radical land reforms".

Pointing out that the power sector constitutes the most crucial infrastructure both for agriculture and industry, he said that the problems of power must be carefully handled in a co-ordinated fashion with due attention for the proper choice of fuels, the adequacy of their availability, the need to rationalize tariff structure, and to prevent transmission and distribution losses.

In fact, the problem of power may reach crisis proportions in the next few years unless urgent action is taken by every state. The financial, managerial and administrative structue of State Electricity Boards (SEBs) and their policies must be changed dramatically and urgently so that the Electricity Boards can raise tariffs to realistic levels, improve the quality of supply, contain power theft and become financially viable. The Finance Minister, Mr. P. Chidambaram, is of the view that the Central and State laws need to be changed to allow SEBs and private electricity companies to function autonomously subject to independent regulatory authorities.

In respect of sectoral strategies, the document emphasizes that agriculture has a vital place in the economic development of the country as it contributes 29.4 per cent of GDP and employs about 64 per cent of the workforce. There has been a significant improvement in agricultural productivity which has helped in reducing rural poverty. It is noted that capital formation (at 1980-81 prices) in agriculture grew at tha rate of 6.05 per cent during 1989-90 to 1994-95. In the accelerated growth scenario for the Ninth Plan, efforts will need to be made to achieve an agricultural growth rate of 4.5 per cent per annum in contrast with 3.5 per cent growth rate during the Eighth Plan period on an average.

The role of basic inputs in agriculture cannot be underestimated. Timely and adequate availabilty of inputs for agriculture and agriculture-related infrastructure will need to receive special attention. Therefore, regional programmes have to be formulated in such a manner as to ensure provision of inputs to the farmer, particularly in the remote, hilly, backward and tribal areas. Likewise, augmentation of irrigation facilities is necessary to increase the gross cropped areas even under rainfed vonditions and invreasing cropping intensity in agriculture areas and assinging priority ot the completion of ongoing projects—both major and minor irrigation.

Another vital input is rural credit. Greater credit flow will be ensured to meet the investment requirements of the farming community for stepping up the growth of production. The approach paper of the Plan stresses that efforts would be made to ensure timely and adequate availability of credit, particularly to small and marginal farmers and tribal farmers at reasonable rates so as to enable them to make investments necessary for higher production. More importantly, the crop insurance scheme is going to receive a big thrust for providing security to marginal and small farmers in rainfed areas during the Ninth Plan period.

Referring to the controversy over poverty estimates exercise, Prof. Dandavate points out that a group in the Plan panes has smoothed out some 'kinks' in the poverty estimate arising out of the appliation of the Lakadwala Committee methodology. He said that the group has suggested that in assessing rural poverty, the agricultural labourers' consumer price index should be used and for estimating urban poverty, the industrial workers' consumer price index should be untilized for updating the poverty line. It is hoped that the Planning Commission would finally decide on this issue during the final draft of the Plan.

Unlike the Eight Five Year Plan of which the structural framework claimed more than a three-year time under the exercise of repeatedly reconstituted Planning Commission by as many as three Prime Ministers appearing in the see-saw political scene since 1989 to get itself approved in May 1992, the approach paper to the Ninth Five Year Plan has happily received approval of the National Development Council on 16 January, 1997 which still leaves two-and-half-month period to complete the tenure of the current Plan. The approach paper to the Ninth Plan, now available, will reap the benefit of being commented upon widely in various media. This is a definite advantage and, if everything goes well, the Ninth Plan comprising the period from 1 April, 1997 to 31 March, 2002 will take off in time without suffering a delay like the pre-Eighth Plan two-year plan holiday.

The approach to the Ninth Plan is undoubtedly bold and highly ambitious. The Plan envisages an annual economic growth rate of seven per cent per annum with an increase of savings and investment rates of 26.2 per cent and 28 per cent respectively, within the limit of ceiling on current account deficit at 2.4 per cent of GDP. The Prime Minister, Mr H.D. Deve Gowda had called for collective efforts to raise the huge resource quantum of Rs. 8,75,000 crore for implementing the Plan.

The approach paper to the Ninth Plan does initiate a departure from traditional lines of the past in more than one way.

First, the States are being given a wider latitude in the affairs of rural development under a basket of programmes complex with, however, an added responsibility of mobilizing additional funds.

Secondly, the role of government has been deeply examined against the backdrop of a fast-changing economic scenario and emerging dynamism in the international politico-economic horizon that is increasingly necessitating a larger role of the private sector.

Thirdly, the role of involvement of people in the

process of nation building through of nation building through decentralized planning has received deeper attention than in the VIII Plan.

Fourthly, the question of growth with social justice and equity has received greater focus with stock taking of achievements in the areas of basic minimum services and a renewed emphasis on quick realization of the remaining tasks.

Fifthly, the need for an effective family welfare and population policy has been spelt out as an indispensable factor in the planning process and the employment generation target is aimed at eight million jobs per year with the emphasis on high employment-elastic activities in the agro-allied areas of animal husbandry, fishery, horticulture, dairy farming, fish preservation and the like.

The important thrust areas as highlighted in the approach paper are agriculture, infrastructure and the social sector areas which have by and large remained neglected during the VIII Plan. The Ninth Plan expects to achieve an agricultural growth rate of 4.5 per cent annually which is looked upon as a chief engine of poverty removal and rural development. Though the output of agricultural sector during the VIII Plan grew by 3.5 per cent per annum, the approach paper expects that a higher rate of public investment in irrigation, soil conservation, flood and drought preventive measures, marketing infrastructure and in sectoral diversification to high value crops will achieve the Ninth Plan target of 4.5 per cent of annual output growth.

The loss of community reality and participation jeopardize many values of the democratic tradition. Those generous impulses that grow out of an awareness of a local common good are weakened. One is merely lost in the amorphous anonymity of a huge population.

As a consequence, the ordinary citizen becomes less and less articulate and makes fewer contributions to the decisions that shape his own destiny or the collective destiny. The democratic experience, whereby the voice of the ordinary citizens at the local grass roots has been heard in higher-level decisions, is lost. So a method of work that promises to increase the responsibility of the citizens, is pertinent to the treatment of the malaise of our time.

Much of the literature on community development is more expressive of the writer's enthusiasm to do good than of any discipline of description and evaluation. Both the enthusiasm and discipline are necessary if this field of work with people is even to approach the fulfillment of its promise,

As to values, let it be stated immediately that development is always normative. That is, it takes place in the midst of actions that serve chosen goals. No scientist (social or any other kind), when he takes part in development, can be content with description only. He must approve actions and evaluate results in the light of some scheme of values towards the attainment of which the development is directed. The paradox for the scientist is that he will never describe man as he is. He will need also to describe man in the process of becoming and this latter task requires planned development that seeks chosen goals.

In regard to community development and people's participation, the emerging consensus clusters round a concept of the improvement of people, the underprivileged, the overprivileged, and all in between. Improvement is evaluated in terms of democratic skills, responsibility to serve growing awareness of a common good, ethical sensitivity, and willingness to co-operate. All other improvements are judged good or bad by reference to what is happening to the people involved.

In the preceding paragraphs we have emphasized upon some value loaded normative ideas which may appear like Utopia but they are the sine qua non of all the development strategy. If we look into the successive Five Year Plan documents from the I Plan to the VIII Plan, it is evident that by and large they have been laudable and reflected the pious dreams of the founding fathers of the nation. However, on the performance side, we have always drawn, if not blank, at least little achievements. The Ninth Plan document emphasizes more on rural infrastructure, the social sector and equity, which are based on the Common Minimum Programme of the United Front government. No doubt, the approach is very laudable but again it is a million dollar question as to what we will achieve at the end of the Ninth Five Year Plan. Instead of lamenting over this question, in the succeeding pages the approach to Ninth Five Year Plan is being discussed in brief and finally our observations on various aspects of the approach paper are given.

It is some satisfication that six years after the so-called "revolution" of liberalization and globalization, we are still talking of planning the growth of the Indian economy. At one stage, the chorus in favour of the miracles of the market was so loud, that one thought that one could just sit back and hope that growth, employment generation, poverty removal, internal and external price stability and social justice, all would just automatically come along one after another in easy succession or even simultaneously, and the Planning Commission would become and anachronism and wither away!

Planning did not, of course, produce any miracle. But it did emphasize the fact that investment in the areas of national priority such as capital goods and infrastructure needed to be substantially raised if the economy was to maximize its rate of growth of national income. In fact, about 80 per cent of public sector investment were directed at achieving that objective. There was bureaucratic red tape, there was a poor work ethos, there was corruption but there was no fault in the objective and none, therefore, in the rationale for having a planned mixed economy in the country.

The Ninth Plan seems to be veering round to that view after we lost six precious years in the wake of the "revolution". But it is still not doing that with the conviction which had gone with the earlier plans barring the last one. The Eighth Plan fumbled with indicative versus target planning with a greater focus on indicative posture particularly in respect of the corporate industrial sector on which much globalization has remained focused. The consequence of that fumbling has been the mounting arrears of investment in infrastructure even after the controversial sop of counter-guarantees was offered to some foreign investors. Whether the Ninth Plan has been forewarned about the total inadequacy of foreign private investment in Indian infrastructure at least on the basis of the Eighth Plan experience, is unclear. But if seeks to go on repeating emphasis in that investment, thus trying to be a mere 'facilitator' rather than 'doer' in the infrastructure sector, it may end up with a much lower rate of growth than seven per cent; what is worse, it may produce a more undesirable content of economic growth than hitherto. The earlier rate of growth of durable consumer goods was 12 per cent plus and the new one could be 17 per cent plus. Will that be regarded as enriching the growth content in a poor country particularly when the infrastructure growth is hardly exceeding three per cent per annum!

Thus while we welcome the Ninth Plan's

commitment to seven per cent rate of growth of output, we are unclear now with an obsession for the great prowess of the foreign investor, and a gradual abandonment of the role of the State as a doer in place of that of the facilitator, even in the infrastructure sector, the commitment will be carried through.

Since there is in this a danger that the invisible preference for indicative planning which was in evidence in some parts of the Eighth Plan is brought forward to the Ninth Plan as well, a word about the relevance of this type of planning might be in order here.

Indicative planning is an attempt by the Planning Authority to project relative demands and supplies of goods with some given time horizon in mind. Its aim is to plan in a manner that market players and also the State, if it too is amongst them, are enabled to prevent falling into an excess or deficient demand situation. It is expected to assist a balanced allocation of resources in the economy.

Assuming that the purpose of planning is to augment supplies of infrastructure, capital goods, technology, wage goods, national security and a pollution-free growth, (these priorities have remained crucial throughout the planning period and should remain so in the Ninth Plan as well), how will mere indication of supply deficiencies meet our purpose? The hope that once the deficiencies are identifies, the local or foreign private investors could be induced to remove them is sheer bravado. The growth of infrastructure in terms of market rules raises a host of issues beginning with the rate of return and ending with the entire ques tion of external economy if private investors insisting on adequate risk coverage and a smaller time horizon for recovery of their fixed capotal investments, charge exhorbitant prices for that infrastructure. Further, the resulting higher prices of infrastructure services may turn out to be antipeople. The tendency of the market to raise prices in areas of scarcity (and infrastructure is such an area) is unavoidable. As for governmental control and regulation of monopolist price fixing, brought in against privately run infrastructure, there could be the same type of problems which have been generally used to decry governmental role in economic activities.

India's development goals—growth with social justice and self-reliance, with particular emphasis on eradication of poverty and human development—have remained more or less unchanged throughout the plan period since 1951. Early strategies for achieving these goals entailed large investments in the public sector for infrastructure development and creation of industrual base, regulation and licensing of the privae sector to channelize investments into priority areas, import restrictions to protect the domestic industries and limitations to foreign investments.

Social justice was expected to result from economic growth as well as through direct including health, education, etc. While these strategies had helped in creating an industrial base and self-sufficiency in food production, they did not lead to a pattern of develoment and growth rates sufficient enough to eradicat poverty and achieve social justice.

Shift in strategy

The need for a shift in strategy to a competitive industrial environment and open trade regime was recognized for quite some time. The attempts made in the eighties were, however, too feeble to make a significant impace. A shift in economic strategy towards a more openand more competitibve economy began in 1991 in the aftermath of severe macro-economic imbalances particularly in the balance of payments situation and in the fical position of the government.

There was also a growing recognition that much more attention was needed to addres human development in all its many facets to achieve broad-based economic growth along with equity and social justice. The experience of fast growin East Asian countries where human development precede ecnomic growth underscored the importance of investment in human development. The experience of these countries, further, highlights the fact that the gains from economic growth gets widely distributed via employment and this can be facilitated by universal primary of widespread skills.

The economic reforms initiated in 1991 included stablilization measures and structural adjustment policies. Besides, fiscal and exchange rate correction, the measures included deregulation of industry, partial disinvestment of public sector enterprises, encoragement of foreign investment—both direct and portfolio, liberalization of foreign trade and an array of measures to achieve structural reform of institutions in the financial sector and capitctor and captial markets. The reforms strategy also included measures to promote employment opportunities in agriculture, industry and social sectors. A number of target-oriented programmess aimed at poverty alleviation and provision of vasic minimum social services to the poor also got strengthened.

The VIII Plan (1992-97) formulated in the wake of introduction of the reforms strategy attempted to imbibe the ethos of the reforms. But in its detailed structural characterixtics it was broadly as continuation of the earlier plans. Theis has resulted in several constraints in the implementation of the VIII Plan and also. perhaps, decelerated the progress of economic reforms.

In the approach to the Ninth Five Year Plan (1997-

2002), it is realized that the growth pattern of the VII Plan (1992-97) did not benefit the poor and the underprivileged. The Ninth Plan, therefore, contemplates to usher in a new era of people, oriented planning in which the government and the people, particularly the poor, can fully participate. Though this participatory planning process, it is expected to ensure equity and accelerate the rate of growth of the economy and thus raise the agricultural and rural incomes and to target these with programmes which aim at small, medium, and marginal farmers and landless labourers. Provision of irrigation water and inputs on a widespread basis in different agro-climatic regions of the country, backed by suitable policy measures for creating infrastructure, would be the most important the creation of adequate employment opportunities through a broad-based programme of development and economic growth.

These need to be accompanied by measures which (BMSs) such as sage drinking water, availability of primary health service facilities, universalisation of primary education, provision of public housing assistance to all shelterless poor families, nutritional support to children, connectivity of all villages and habitations by roads, and public distribution system targeted to the poor. While the objectives of this programme have been decided through mutual consultation, the States have been give full opportunity to decide on the phasing of the target for each specific sector. The achievement of these targets would be jointly monitored by the State and the Central governments.

This approach is an ideal blends of national commitments with local initiatives. In addition, the process of development that is being contemplated would empower all the disadvantaged sections of the population, especially the Scheduled Castes (SCs), and minorities to integrate them in the mainstream. Besides, women and children and the physically handicapped and disabled are also vulnerable. Fore these sections of society, planned State intervention would be required in order to provide them with adequate opportunities for education and employment in an attempt to involve them productively in the development process. Above all the role of the government would be to facilitate the process of peoplè's involvement by creating right types of institutional infrastructure, particularly in rural areas. Panchayati Raj bodies in rural areas are to be directly involved in the development process and people's involvement through their elected representatives would be realized. Cooperatives would be strengthened and self-help groups, association of workers/producers, etc. encouraged. The government would seek active partnership with the voluntary sector in organizing and promoting these institutions. In the light of the foregoing discussion and in the context of four important dimensions of State policy, viz quality of life, generation productive employment, regional imbalance, and self-reliance, the approach paper spells out the following objective:

— Priority to agriculture and rural development with a view to generating adequate productive employment and eradication;

— Accelerating the growth rate of the economy with stable prices;

— Ensuring food and nutritional security for all, particularly the vulnerable sections of society;

— Providing the basic minimum services of sage drinking water, primary health care facilities, universal primary education, shelter, and road connectivity to all habitations in a time-bound manner;

— Containing the growth rate of population;

— Ensuring environmental sustainability of the development process through social mobilization and participation of people at all levels;

— Empowerment of women and socially disadvantaged groups such as SCs, STs, OBCs, and minorities as agents of socio-economic change and development;

— Promoting and developing people's participatory institutions like Panchayati Raj bodies, co-operatives, and self-help groups; and

— Strengthening efforts to build self-reliance.

The approach paper adopted by the National Development Council on 16 January, 1997 envisages a seven per cent annual growth rate in Gross Domestic Product (GDP) as against the 5.9 per cent GDP likely to be achieved during the VIII Plan. It is assumed by the Planning Commission that domestic savings can be pushed up from the current level of 23.7 per cent GDP to 26.2 per cent. This is based on the optimistic belief that government expenditure reduction can be effected bringing down the budgetary deficit and mobilizing resources by public sector enterprises.

The Finance Ministry has been cautious and favoured a 6.2 per cent GDP growth rate with a public sector outlay of Rs. 20,04,000 crore. Even budgetary support for the plan cannot be more than Rs. 3,00,000 crore. But he figure has been fixed at Rs. 3,70,000 crore with a higher level of taxation of corporate profit etc.

There are three related aspects which make the tasks of Ninth Plan formulation and implementation difficult.

First, a higher percentage of population below the poverty line, i.e., 37.27 per cent of population in 1993—94 has to be taken care of in anti–poverty programmes in the place of 16.82 per cent assumed by the earlier government. This will call for more resources. It is curious to note that between 1987–88 and 1993–94, rural poverty has gone down only to a small extent even though agricultural growth has been high. But in the later period, when agriculture growth was not high, rural poverty has gone down to a much greater extent. This is an evidence of the fact that agricultural development alone is not–sufficient for rural development and poverty removal.

Secondly, the growth rate of agriculture is envisaged to be 4.5 per cent it is doubtful whether this can be achieved unless there is adequate thrust on both fiscal and human resource inputs. That is why the local resource mobilization strategy has to give a prominent place to human resource development investment like education, health, nutrition, etc.

Thirdly, the saving as a percentage of GDP over 26 per cent may be on the high side and, therefore, labour will have to be used as a substitute for the limited capital.

When there is local planning and local resource mobilization, the objective of rural development can be achieved with accelerated growth of agriculture and its productivity. In fact, in the case of rural societies like what we have in India, rural development will imply also social change and rural transformation as well as development. All these are complementary to each other in several ways for accelerating the pace of rrural development.

It has been found that there can be growth in literacy, which is a prerequisite for rural development, when educational facilities, communication facilities, communicable roads and access to electricity are improved.

The issues we now have to consider are: (a) Why there are such unutilized resources in the rural areas; (b) how real are the opportunities for such local resource mobilization; (c) In the process of such mobilization how rural development can take place; and (d) What is the role of human resources development in this process. It is the contention of this paper that when there is a shortage of resources at the macro—level for implementing the plan, additional resources are best mobilized at the local level. In the very process of mobilizaton of non—financial resources, new oportunities for meeting localy perceived needs will be found and exploited.

The first novelty of the Ninth Plan is that the Planning Commission has decided to give more freedom to the State governments in formulating their plans. The Planning Commission has decided that in consultation with the Union Ministry of Finance, it will indicate the probable amount of Central assistance available to each State and the State governments would be left free to determine the size of their plans. It may be recalled in this context that the earlier practice followed was that the State governments would propose specific size of the States' annual plans. The Planning Commission would scrutinize them in detail and then extract a promise of additional resource mobilization from the States before approving the plan size. This gave unnecessary credibility to the size of the States' plans. Every state would push the plan size to unrealistically high level hoping that the Planning Commission would provide additional plan assistance. This never happened. As a result, many States used to reduce their plans by December each year and wide gaps used to emerge between the original plan size and the final actual plan. What is more, the plan size came to be politicized at the State level. Nobody would accept the size of the plan lesser than the previous years' and it had to be necessarily higher at least by 10 per cent. This kind of politicisation has been removed during the Ninth Five Year Plan period. The Planning Commission indicates the gross and net plan assistance available to each State and leaves the final size of the plan to be determined by the State government depending upon its capacity to raise additional revenue. This is the first change in the process of planning introduced by the Planning Commission during the Ninth Five Year Plan period.

The second change is that while determining the Central assistance to the State plans, the financial resources which used to flow from the financial institutions like LIC/NABARD/IDB/GIC plus statutory liquidity ratio (SLR) market borrowings were treated as Central government transfers. Though the Central government has control over the borrowing powers of the State governments, particularly when they are indebted to the Central government, these sources of funds are the prerogative of the State governments. The State governments are free to raise funds through banks and other financial institutions depending upon the financial viability of the projects and their capacity to service the debt. However the Planning Commission and the Union Ministry of Finance have evolved a unified borrowing policy to protect the interests of poorer States and minimise the adverse impact of public borrowing on the economy. Therefore, these financial institutions were asked to co-ordinate their direct lending to the State governments. In this ways, the Planning Commission used to treat SLR and other such borrowings from the developmental financial institutions as part of Central assistance. This practice was disliked by States like West Bengal an, therefore, the Planning Commission has now changed the accounting format in such a way as to show institutional finance and SLR borrowing as States' own resources available for plan purpose. This does not change the resource position of the States in any way. But it goes a long way in giving them and they need not be at the mercy of the Central government to raise funds from lending institutions.

Thirdly, for the first time the approach paper recognized the federal nature of the Indian planning system and has devoted a separate chapter explaining how the Planning Commission is going to decentralize not merely plan formaulation but also the entire planning process including monitoring of implementation. The document recognizes the implications of the far-reaching political change that has taken place in India. From the inception of the planning regime, the Central government used to be formed by a national party which used to dictate terms to the state governments But in the 1996 elections, no national party secured a majority and a number of regional parties have joined hands to form the United Front government at the Centre. This is an unprecedented change in the political scenario. Consequently, the Planning Commision's thinking had to reflect this changed situation and give more voice to the State governments in the planning process. At the same time, the State governments are made to realize that they have to mobilize adequate additional resources and harmonize their budgets with a view to reducing fiscal imbalance in the economy.

Furthermore, the Planning Commission has been persuading the Central ministries to transfer a large number of Centrally-sponsored schemes (CSS) along with the corresponding funds to the State governments so that the Central domination in the development process and priorities of the States is reduced. For instance, about 1823 Centrally-sponsored schemes with an outlay of Rs. 16,038. 19 crore were being implemented during the Eighth Plan period. The Chief Minister's conference held in July, 1996 expressed the view that the number of CSS should be reduced and transferred to the States. But the Central ministers are reluctant to transfer many schemes. They agreed to transfer the schemes worth Rs. 1,300 crore only. Therefore, the Planning Commission has taken the initiative and is persuading the Central ministries to transfer more schemes along with the funds to the State governments as per the decision of the NDC which has laid down that CSS outlay sould not exceed one-sixth of total Central assistance. In 1979-80, 71 CSS were transferred to the states with an outlay of Rs. 2,000 crore. While this is not a new phenomenon as it was done earlier also, it still augurs well for the States autonomy. The only occasion when it was done on a large scale was during the Janata Party rule which again gave prominence to true federal structure in the planning process.

The reconstituted Planning Commission believes that the principal task of planning in the post-reform era in our federal framework is to evolve a shared vision of and a shared commitment to the national objectives and the development strategy not only in the government at all levesl but also among all economic agents. The principal objective of the Ninth Plan is to build on the succsses of the VIII Plan, whike tackling the problems that have emerged, particularly in agriculture, living standard of the poor, infrastructure, social sector, regional disparity and fiscal deficits. The IX Plan will facilitate broadening and deepening the economic reforms process to ensure that the fruits of development reach the backward regions of the country and benefit the poorer sections of the society in a time-bound manner.

Provision of BMSs: The conference of State Chief Ministers held in july 1996 made a commitment to provide seven basic minimum services universally by AD 2000. They are (i) safe drinking water, (ii) access to primary health care, (iii) universal primary education, (iv) public housing assistance for the homeless, (v) extension of the midday meal scheme, (vi) road connectivity to all villages, and (vii) food security through the public distribution system for all families below the poverty line. The IX Plan will attempt to operationalize this commitment.

The approach to the IX Plan outlines a long-term fiscal policy stance indicating methods by which resources of the governments at all levels can be augmented in order to reduce and eventually eliminate the revenue deficit at all levels.

Along with aggregate economic growth, balanced regional development has been an essential component of our development strategy from the inception of planning. since not all regions of the country are well-endowed or equipped to take advantage of the growth objectives provided by the market, planned intervention continues to be essential to ensure reduction in regional imbalances.

Care for the poor: Our society continues to have a sizeable number of members who still suffer from abject poverty and deprivation. A vast majority of them do not get an opportunity to participate in the market economy. They are neither able to contribute nor receive anytying from the market process. Special employment programmes to ensure adequate incomes for these sections of the society will continue to be an integral part of the IX Plan. Fruther, appropriate public policies including skill-endowment to the market economy will be part of the Plan.

Uplift of weaker section: Increasing the welfare of the socially and ecnonmically disadvantaged groups, including the Scheduled Castes, Scheduled Tribes and backward classes as well as minorities, handicapped and disabled and women and children is another objective of the Ninth Plan. Planned State intervention is essentisal in order to provide these groups with adequate opportunities for education and employment to enable them to participate productively in the development process.

The main thrust of the Ninth Plan has been to evolve a shared vision of and a shared commitment to the national objectives and the development strategy not only in the government at all levels but also among all other economic agents. No development strategy can be successful unless each component of the economy works towards a common goal and purpose with the full realisation of the role that has to be played within an overall structure of responsibilities. Some of the tasks needed in respect of rural development are given below:

— The principal task during the Ninth Plan, therefore, is to build on the Eighth Plan, while tackling the problems that have emerged, particularly in areas such as capital formation in agriculture, social sector, regional disparity, and fiscal deficits. Indian economy is still vulnerable and the operation of a more open economic system has to be tempered by judicious public interventions to ensure that these vulnerabilities are gradually overcome.

— Since the planning is done for the entire nation, the strategies for resource augmentation need to cover not only the government at all levels but also those which would be available to other sections of the people.

— Since not all parts of the country are equally endowed to take advantage of growth opportunities, planned intervention is needed to ensure that large imbalances do not occur .

— The Indian economy still has a large number of its citizens who live in acute poverty both in rural and urban areas. Special employment programmes targeted to these people will continue in the Ninth Plan. Special attention will need to be paid to unorganized labour, particularly the agricultural landless labourer.

— There exist large disparities across the various social groups. The disadvantaged groups include members belonging to Scheduled Castes and Scheduled Tribes, other backward classes and minorities. In addition, women and children and the physically handicapped and disabled are also vulnerable. For these sections of society State intervention is required in order to provide them with adequate opportunities for education and employment in an attempt to involve them productively in the development process.

— It is heartening to note that the Plan has identified people's initiative and participation as a "key element" in the process of development, particularly in improving the effectiveness of development outlays which has been declining over the years. It has also recognized that the role of the government should be to facilitate the process of people's involvement by creating the right type of institutional infrastructure, particularly in rural areas. The progress on this front so far has not been entirely satisfactory primarily due to the fact that the other tiers of the government were not fully integrated into the development strategy. The Plan also asserts that the process of social mobilization and development of people's initiatives cannot be achieved without the active support and involvement of the political system at all levels. In the Plan, the Panchayati Raj bodies in rural areas will be directly involved in the development process. People's involvement via their elected representatives will be realized through "democratic—decentralization".

— Co-operatives will be rejuvenated to enlist people's active participation in these societies. They will be liberated from tight bureaucratic control. Self-help groups, associations of workers or small producers, etc. are other forms of institutions which will be encouraged to actively involve people in planning process and implementation. Government will seek active "partnership" with the voluntary sector in organizing and promoting these institutions.

— Domestic entrepreneurship, which is the backbone of the development process, will be fully encouraged through measures to enhance their competitive strength and to facilitate their growth and efficiency. In particular, the small-scale and village and home industries will be provided the proper environment for growth and diversification.

— While new initiatives are being taken for additional investment, optimum utilization of the existing infrastructure should not be neglected. This needs to be done by technology upgradation, systems improvement and ensuring public utilities function on commercial lines. Most importantly, care should be taken to ensure that in the provision of these services, the rural areas are provided their due share both in terms of magnitude as well as technology suited to their needs.

— In regard to subsidies, emphasis is laid to move to a system of transparent subsidies directed towards specific target-groups in a selective manner.

— The Indian Planning process had always laid emphasis on measures to ensure sustainability of the development process not only in economic terms, but also in terms of social and environmental factors. The Ninth Plan will carry this tradition further and consolidate on the creation of conditions for sustainable development.

In the background of the foregoing discussions, the following points become very relevant:

— A plan is not merely a reflection of desires. but is equally a statement of possibles, the extent to which it is possible to fulfil the felt needs within the available human, material, and financial resources in a given time-frame. It is basically an efficient management of the scarce resources for which structures are created. Integrated planning needs integrated machinery for development. Plan formulation, plan administration, and plan evaluation go as a continuous planning process.

— Planning is for the people and, therefore, it has to be of the people and by the people —People's participation has to be secured and sustained—a clear departure from the concept of charity to the concept of involvement so that development is achieved by a process which affords opportunities for the people to participate in the formulation and implementation of plans through a system of open and democrtic decision-making. This will take care of, what has been remarked as, over-centralization in planning, over-bureaucratization in implementaion, and fragmentation at the field-level which leads to over-dependence of the people on the government.

— Choice of schemes has to be strictly in accordance with the pepole's own perception of their problems and their needs. Left to themselves people choose to saitisfy infrastructural and immediate physical needs (security against hunger) firstly, followed by satisfaction of other needs. Thus, given an assured opportunity, people can themselves create assets of great value and utility with minimum expenditure. They voluntarily contribute to the labour and material when it comes to the satisfaction of their left needs. What is needed today is a successful co-operative partnership between the people for all-round development of the people living in every village irrespective of its location. A concept of joint management is to emerge.

Relationship between democracy and development can thus only be institutionalized at the level of people themselves. This will further forge a partnership between the Gram Panchayat and the government machinery. Once this is achieved, a satisfactory and equitable system of sharing the gains and pains of development can be successfully achieved and 'operation by the people and co-operation by the government' promoted. With the passage of the Constitution (Seventy-third Amendment) Bill, 1992 this situation is likely to emerge shortly.

— What is most urgently needed is the skill for plannig at different leels (Zilla Parishad, Pandchayat Samiti, and Gram Panchayats) of development, so that the needs are properly comprehended, objectives and goals pragmaticaly set, strategies suitably developed, schemes properly formulated, resources efficiently mobilized, and targets seccessfully achieved. The pertinent issue, therfore, which needs to be closely looked into is: How to impart skill in the planning process (plan formulation, plan administration, and plan evaluation) particalarly at the district level and below?

Assumptions
In the light of the above, the following three assumptions need special attention:

— People are at various levels of socio-economic and cultural development and thus have varied problems. When the problems are different, there connot be a fixed or rigid approach to their development;

— A programme is acceptable to a people on a sustainable basis only when it is economical and appealing to them; and

— Poverty and unemployment are primarily due to incapabilities of individuals and groups. Such incapabilities have three dimensions:

(a) Lack of comperhension;

(b) Lack of competence; and

(c) Lack of confidence.

These have also to be developed suitably in order to acheve the benefits of rural development during the Ninth Plan.

The Ninth Five Year Plan (1997-2002) has the strategy to achieve a seven per cent growth rate for the economy. The approach paper for the Plan was recently endorsed by the National Development Council (NDC) with its final approach paper'would now be put up for public debate before the final document is ready and implemented from 1 April, 1997.

The seven per cent growth in gross domestic product (GDP) would be through a 9.3 per cent annual growth in industrial production, 4.5 per cent growth in agriculture, while the fiscal deficit is to be brought down to four per cent of GDP. The approach document has sought an increase in gross domestic savings rate from the Eighth Plan average of 23.7 per cent to 26.2 per cent in the Ninth Plan. The gap between investment needs and domestic savings can be bridged through increased inflow of foreign capital.

Objectives

"Growth with equity" has been adopted as the theme of the Plan. The followint are the main objectives to be fulfilled during the Plan period:

— Generation of adequate productive employment and eradication of poverty.

— Acceleration in the growth rate of the economy with stable price.

— Provision for basic minimum services of safe drinking water, primary health care facilities, universal primary education, shelter and connectivity to all villages in a time-bound manner.

— Ensuring food and nutritional security for all, particularly the vulnerable sections of society.

— Containing the growth rate of population.

— Ensuring environmental sustainability of the development process through socila mobilization and participation of people at all levels.

— Empowerment of women and socially disadvantaged groups as agents of socio-economic change and development.

— Promoting and developing people's participatory institutions like Panchayati Raj bodies, co-operatives and self-help groups.

— Strengthening efforts to build self-reliance.

The Eighth Plan had identified "human development" as its main focus. The objectives of the Ninth Plan arising from the Common Minimum Programme of the United front government, the Chief Ministers' Conference on basic minimum services and the suggestions that have been put forward by Chief Ministers of various states during extensive consultations are as follows:

Alleviation of rural poverty has been one of the primary objectives of planned development in India. Ever since the inception of planning, the policies and the programmes have been designed and redesigned with this aim. As such, in the Ninth Plan emphasis has been laid on agriculture and rural development with a view to generating adequate productive employment and eradicating poverty.

Secondly, the draft approach paper of the Ninth Plan aims at a higher growth rate of seven per cent per annum as against the average 5.9 per cent (at market prices) of Gross Domestic Product in the Eighth Plan with its main focus being "growth with equity and distributive justice".

Thirdly, the Ninth Plan also seeks empowerment of women and socially disadvantaged groups such as SCs, STs and OBCs and minorities as agents of socio-economic change and development. It also aims at promoting and developing people's participatory institutions like Panchayati Raj, co-operatives and a large number of self-help groups which have been doing yeoman service in developing the potential of the people.

Fourthly, the Ninth Plan aims at ensuring environmental sustainability of the development process through social mobilization and participation of people at all levels.

Fifthly, the Ninth Plan envisages an employment-oriented growth strategy and an appropriate mix of capital and labour and technology which would lead to efficiency of efficiency of these of resources and ensure higher growth for the economy.

Sixthly, the Ninth Plan gives highest priority to provide the seven basic minimum services of safe drinking water, primary health care facilities, universal primary education, shelter, midday meals, connectivity of villages and revitalizing the public distribution system in a time-bound manner.

Finally, it aims at ensuring food and nutritional security for all, particularly the vulnerable sections of society.

The above stated objectives need to be seen in the context of four important dimensions of state policy, viz (a) quality of life of the citizens; (b) generation of productive employment; (c) regional balance; and (d) self-reliance.

Quality of life is multi-dimensional. It encompasses not only the economic opportunities available to the people, but also their ability to take advantage of these opportunities, and the existence of living conditions which permit a healthy and productive life. Eradication of poverty and provision of basic minimum services are integral elements of any strategy to improve the quality of life. No developmental process can be sustainable unless it leads to visible and wide spread improvement in these areas. The problem of shelter for the poor both in urban and rural areas is particularly acute. Thus, a programme of providing assistance for construction of houses needs to be implemented. The above objectives cannot be achieved merely through increased investment, but a significant change in social attitudes and behavioural responses of the people is required. In this process, the role of women is critical. The process of empowerment of women at the political level has already begun, but it needs to be carried forward into the social and economic spheres as well.

To solve the problem of people's access to basic nutritional requirements, the Ninth Plan will lay emphasis on developing strategies by which the problem can be overcome by integrating the food production and distribution systems with the employment and poverty alleviation programmes. In particular, the public distribution system will be restructured in order to provide food grains at substantially lower prices to the poor in a focused manner and to ensure availability of such commodities in the remote and deficit areas of the country.

One of the objectives of the Ninth plan will be to generate greater productive employment in the growth process itself. During the last decade, there has been relatively rapid growth which generated adequate employment opportunities. However, the quality of employment in terms of the incomes received and the work environment leave much to be desired. Thus, it becomes necessary to shift the focus of employment strategies towards creating conditions whereby employment opportunities lead to significantly better living and working conditions of the people and upholding the dignity of labour. Free and compulsory education of children supported by an adequate midday meal programme in schools is the first step towards this end.

Regional balance

The issue of regional balance operates at both the inter-State and the intra-State levels. There is, therefore, the need to address it in a framework that is more flexible than the political and administrative boundaries of each individual State. The focus regarding the issue of regional balance has traditionally been of industrialization. However, reduction in regional disparities, may be better achieved through greater focus on agriculture and other rural activities. As such, it becomes necessary not only to increase the productivity of agriculture in backward areas, but also to increase the degree of integration between the rural areas and the rest of the country through improved connectivity in terms of transport and communications.

Relevance

"Human Development" had been identified as the main focus in the Eighth Plan. This continues to be the main concern of the Ninth Plan also. The objectives of the Plan are deduced from the Common Minimum Programme (CMP) of the United Front government and the Chief ministers' Conference on basic minimum services as well as extensive consultation with the Chief Ministers of various States. Of the nine objectives identified, in keeping with the figure of Ninth Plan, the first objective lays stress rightly on rural development. The objectives are as follows:

— Priority to agriculture and rural development with a view to generating adequate productive employment and eradication of poverty;

— Accelerating growth rate of the economy with stable prices;

— Ensuring food and nutritional security for all sections of society;

— Providing the basic minimum services of safe drinking water, primary heath care facilities, universal primary education, shelter and connectivity to all in a time-bound manner;

— Containing the growth rate of population;

— Ensuring environmental sustainability of the development process through social mobilization and participation of people at all levels.

— Empowerment of women and socially disadvantaged groups such as Scheduled Castes, Scheduled Tribes and other backward classes and minorities as agents of socio-economic change and development.

— Promoting and developing people's participatory institutions like Panchayati Raj bodies, co-operatives and self-help groups;

— Strengthening efforts to build self-reliances.

The emphasis of the above objectives is to seek to achieve "growth with equity and social justice". These have to be seen in the context of four important dimensions of the state policy which are: (a) Quality of life the Citizens; (b) Generation of productive employment; (C) Regional balance; and (d) Self-reliance.

The fear has been expressed by several experts that the New Economic Policy (NEP) of liberalization and globalization is contrary to the basic philosphy of the Indian Five Year Plans which were based to achieve a socialistic pattern of society with active people's participation. People's participation does figure in the Ninth Plan as the key element to achieve the goals of the Plan.

Prof B.M. Bhatia, an economist of considerable standing is of the opinion that the Planning Commission has lost its utility and function in a free-market-economy. The whole exercise of the approach paper according to him was palpably so arithmetical, albeit circular in reasoning, that one wonders whether it could not be left to a schoolboy to do the job instead of the Yojana Bhavan. He further says that the approach paper has failed to spell out concrete policy for social engineering, that is claimed to be the principal objective of the plan. He further asserts that the planners have been very casual in their task as is evident from the fact that the growth rate for the agricultural sector was put at 3.5 per cent which was revised at the instance of the Prime Minister. This would substantially change the whole structure of the Plan as well as the development strategies underlying it. In view of this change, the entire approach paper should have been drasticaly revised and recast. But the planners had neither patience nor the time to do that. They just took 48 hours to raise the agriculture sector growth rate target from the originally envisaged 3.5 per cent to 4.5 per cent. Could there be a better example of a cavalier approach than the one shown by the present Planning Commission in preparing a five year plan for the country.

The Strategy of development adopted in the Ninth Five Year Plan aims at reaching out to those regions and sections of the society which have been bypassed by the process of development. At the same time, it also has to aim at efficiency of resource use in areas and sectors which have already been developed. Supply—side efficiency and technological transformation have to be interwoven with the economic process of increasing the production potential. In order to sustain a growing and well—diversified economy in the Nith Plan, it would be necessary to evolve judicious public policies towards investment and technology, which can mobilize resources that are lying unutilized in the economy and can unleash wider processes of agricultural growth and decentralized developments linked to national and world markets.

Thrust needs to be given to develop modern communication and information system in the villages. Those could be managed and operated by community initiative or growers' association. This would enable the farming community to know about the latest trend of the prices both in the domestic and international market and also quality of food products of other countries, taste and preference of the consumers. Based on the input structure, the output pattern for major crops during the Ninth Plan has been tentatively worked out. In the output projections, adequate emphasis has been laid on relative self—sufficiency in food production, keeping in view the imperative of maintaining food security in the country. In fact, it culd be stated that the Indian economy attained high rates of growth and better economic stability and resilience during the eighties, among other factors, due to the factor of relative food self—sufficiency. It is important to constantly keep this factor in view while chalking out the broad contours of the Ninth Plan.

The State Agricultural Board should construct Haats with necessary infrastructure facilities at important areas/mandis for small and marginal farmers so as to enable them to get rid of dalall agent and sell their agricultural commodities direct to the buyers/consumers. Tis would also generate a number of employment oportunities in the process of marketing activities, besides better price to the farmers. Necessary infrastructure would need to be created in the major growing areas for encouraging the entrepreneurs to set up food processing industries. It would be more appropriate if encouragement is given to joint ventures with growers' participation as members. An agri–business corporation should be set up for marketing the agricultural produce both in the domestic as well as in international markets. The corporation would establish both forward and backward linkages with the growers and help them to improve quality and productivity. For increasing India's share in the world trade of food and food products, modernizaton of agricultural marketing system would need to be encouraged with more emphasis on quality control, sophisticated and eco—friendly packaging and consumer packs.

There is need for flow of investment in dryland agriculture, which is insufficient at present. It can be suggested that if a part of the huge funds allotted in the Ninth Plan for famine relief in the event of drought could be spent for proper nutrition of poor dry land soils and crops, the recurring problem of famines could be solved to a great extent. Given the level of food stocks of the order of 36.4 million tonnes, food avvailibility has ceased to be a constraint on economic development. Also, while due emphasis would continue to be laid on the diversified crop structure in the Ninth Plan, attention would also have to be paid to the development of dairy, poultry, fisheries, friits and vegetables, tea, coffee, rubber plantation, etc. Development of non—crop oriented agricultural activities would involve, inter alia, strengthening of the existing processing facilities for value—addition operations as also installation of new capacities in these fields. During the Ninth Plan, each village information centre will have one Biological Software Library (BSL) to take care of soil health, earthworm farming and biofertilisers production/supply. Thus, this library will provide all types of organic/biotic inputs at the doorsteps of farmers.

Water as a national asset: The special needs of water management and its integration with agricultural operations call for a selective and systematic approach to conjunctive use of water at micro and macro levels. This would help eliminate deterious effects on soil and environment and also help optimize the use of water in crop productivity. There is an urgent need to recognize water as a national asset and its proper utilization whould be a top priority area brooking no delay to increase use–efficiency. Low efficiency of irrigation use ranges from 30 to 70 per cent and there is inequality in distribution of water. Increasing problems of soil salinity, water–logging and soil degradation associated with irrigation are also to be looked into. In working out of the production potential of agriculture during the Ninth Plan, the approach to water development strategies at the subregional level is to be vigorously pursued. This approach sets specific targets for projects like tank irrigation, watershed development, modernization and completion of canal system and diversification of cropping sequences in different agro–climatic regions of India. It is also necessary to strengthen the appropriate input structure of irrigation, fertilizer consumption, crop intensity and crop diversification, etc. for building up the production potential of agriculture during the Ninth Plan.

Emphasis should continue to be laid on the Integrated Watershed Development Projects. Various soil and water conservation technologies need to be energetically pursued to raise productivity in the marginal and rainfed land holdings. As per preliminary estimates, the share of irrigated area in gross sown area is likely to be 48.4 per cent in the terminal year of the Ninth Plan diversified agriculture and crop intensification should be propagated with the crop intensity reaching the level of 1.40 by 2001—2002.

It is necessary that institutional finances as advanced by the co—operative credit system and commercial banks and regional rural banks to the agricultural sector should consistently increase during the Ninth Plan. The priority sector lending target set by government for commercial banks should be fulfilled by all the public sector banks during each year of the Ninth Plan. Such a commitment on the part of institutional financing agencies will considerably help in financing development needs in the agriculture and rural development sectors.

The sectoral allocation of the total investment has to be so designed that investment in agriculture and rural development should get a big push in the Ninth Plan. In the Ninth Plan, out of the total investment, the share of agriculture and rural development needs to be increased to about 30 per cent. This is very important, as in recent years, capital formation in the agricultural sector has tended to decline.

The agricultural sector is likely to have a bright future due to the overall expansion of the economy through liberalization, globalization and privatization. The agricultural production, productivity, export and employment is likely to pick up in the future due to its forward linkages with the economy. At the same time, the liberalized economic environment is expected to show some side—effects on crokpping pattern, income distribution and employment. In the overall context, the Ninth Plan hopes to integrate the planning process for the globalization of agriculture.

The Strategy of Ninth Plan in India Agricultural sector is the following :

— The aim is to make the agriclutural sector grow at the rate of 4.5 per cent per annum.

— A regionally differntiated strategy is to be adopted, based on agronomic, climatic and environmentally—friendly conditions, on the following lines;

(a) North—western high productivity region: The focus will be on (a) promoting diversification of crops with the emphasis on high–value crops, (b) strengthening linkages with the agro–processing industry and exports, and (c) creation of basic infrastructure.

(b) Eastern region with abundant water: Productivity in this region is very low despite availability of abundant water. In order to increase productivity, emphasis will be on flood control, drainage management, improvement of irrigation facilities and input delivery systems, along with adequate agricultural credit and extension services.

(c) Water—scarce region—Peninsular India including Rajasthan: Low productivity in this region is attributed to water scarcity. The focus will be on development of efficient water harvesting and conservation methods, suitable irrigation packages based on watershed approach and promotion of an appropriate farming system.

(d) Ecologically fragile regions including the Himalayasand desert areas: The emphasis is to be on development of ecofriendly agriculture in these areas.

— With respect to basic inputs, regional programmes are to be formulated in such a manner as to ensure timely and adequate availability of inputs to the farmer, particularly in the remote, hilly, backward and tribal areas. The approach as regards inputs is as follows:

(a) Irrigation: Priority is to be given to completion of ongoing major and medium irrigation projects.

(b) Fertilizers: Consumption of fertilizers in low—use areas and crops is to be increased; imbalances in the use of plant nutrients are to be reduced; an integrated pest management system is to be adopted; emphasis is to be given on use of biotic agents. In order to accomplish these tasks, a programme of soil–testing across the various agro—climatic regions is to be initiated. It is recognized that fertilizer imports need to be curtailed, and hence, output and productivity of fertilizer production units should be increased through better capacity utilization, improvement in energy efficiency in order to reduce production costs, and other measures towards the goal of modernizing the fertilizer industry.

(c) Seeds: The focus will be on promoting a higher seed replacement rate. Then, in the post—GATT period, new plant variety protection rights make it necessary to increase facilities for registration of varieties; steps are to be taken in this direction.

(d) Credit: Efforts are to be made to ensure timely and adequate availability of credit, particularly to small and marginal farmers and tribal farmers at reasonable rates, so that they have the wherewithal for making investment, which would step up production levels.

(e) Other issues: Implementation of the National Watershed Development Programme will be intensified for development of rainfed farming areas; the crop insurance scheme will be focused on to provide security to marginal and small farmers in rainfed areas; in every district, the RIDF is to be used to cover projects which encourage groups of small farmers, artisans and landless labourers, in order to facilitate skill upgradation , processing, better transportation and quqality improvement. These projects can be centred around large agro—based projects or identified sources of regional, national and export demand.

Then, research efforts are to be enhanced in the spheres of biotechnology, microbiology, genetic improvement of crops, genetic upgradation of animal resources, etc. Teaching facilities in the area of agricultural education are to be upgraded, and the existing infrastructure for transfer of technology is to be made more effective and responsive to meet the needs of farmers.

This, threrfore, establishes the need for evolving a two–prolonged strategy to raise the level of the productivity per unit area when there is no scope for bringing more area under these crops but to release the part of the existing area to meet other economic needs. The two pronged strategy refers to:

— Adoption of available proven technology by all the farmers in a period of five years.

— Strengthening the basefor research, extension and education so that the integrated approach can create an impact in the future.

Proven technology already demonstrated to farmers revolves around use of high—yielding verietal (HYV) seeds or hybrid seeds, organic manure accompanied by chemicalfertilizers, irrigation or adoption of soil and moisture conservation practices, prevention or control of pests and diseases, farm—machineries, agronomic practices and post—harvrest technology. For all food crops, agricultural universities set up in each of the States as also research institutes of the Indian Council of Agricultural Research (ICAR) have already evolved and standardized a package of practicesfor specific regions or areas which are also demonstrated b them or by the Krishi Vigyan Kendras.

In order to achieve the yield potential, the farmers should be enabled to use HYV or hybrid seeds which under a given dose of fertilizer and moisture can express their full yield potential. In respect of rice, the hybrids released for Andhra Pradesh, Tamil Nadu, Karnataka and West Bengal capable of yielding an additional one to 1.5 tonner per hectarethan the besyt variety, have earned for

India the distinction of being the second country after China to makethe hybrid technology in rice, a field reality. These hybrids, viz APHR188—1, APHR—2, MGR—1, KRH—1, CNHR—3, DRRH—1 and KRH—4 need to be produced and supplied afresh every year to all the farmers in the area of Telengana and Rayalseema, Tamil Nadu, Karnataka and West Bengal, as only afraction of thearea is presently covered in these States under these hybrids. Likewise, a balanced use of fertilizer nutrients inadequate quantities is necessary to increase yield and sustain soil health and productivity levels. Abrupt increase in fertilizer prices and reduction or removal of subsidy on phosphatic and potassic fertilizers have resulted into unbalanced use of nutrients adversely affecting the productivity of the food crops. Also, application of major and minor nutrients should be made after testing the soil which would help increase productivity and resuce the cost. Basal dose of farm yard manure or biogas slurry is a must for maintaining and enhancing inherent soil fertility. All these aspects are at present ignored by farmers which must be ensured through education and monitoring.

The present status of irrigating the crops either throgh canal or well also needs to be improved consederably. Time method and quantum of water according to the varieties of crops, soil and climate have been evolved which should be judiciously followed. Water is a scarce and very costly commodity, which, if judiciously and scientifically used, will also increase productivity of crops and will not have any adverse effect on soils which we have now been experiencing. Not only is there a most urgent need to conserve water through the use of drip and sprinkler irrgation system but the unused potential of about 13.9 million hectares must also be put to judicious use.

Technological breakthrough would only create the expected impact if agricultural operatons right from land preparation to post—harvest opertions are conducted speedily, effectively and on time for which specific types of farm equipment devised by the research, testing and training centres, power and farm machinery divsion of the agricultural universities as also the Central Institute of Agricultural Engineering are popularized, produced and supplied to farmers. Plant protection, though significantly important, has yet not received the needed attention bythe farmers. For this purpose, a campaign on war footing should be mounted so that all farmers adopt the integrated pest management practices in a time—bound programme. Along with this, losses during harvest and post—harvest operations till the food grains reach the consumers have to be prevented or drastically minimized through adoption of methods already developed for this purpose.

Achievements and failures

The late Eric P.W. Da Costa, Editor, Eastern Economist writes that In Indian planning still contains serious defects in statistical method.

He, commenting on the second Five Year Plan, wrote that it was good so far as it was on paper. This may be true of subsequent plans as well (italics added). Da Costa felt that there was no guarantee that its figures were not as full of mistakes and misjudgements as the First Five Year Plan. Consider for example, some of the co-ordinates of First Five Year Plan. National income in the Indian Union in the First Five Year Plan was to rise by 11 per cent. In point of fact, as the draft outline of the Second Five Year Plan had shown, it had risen by 18 per cent. In other words, there was an error of over 50 per cent in these estimates on practically every item, the growth of the economy as a whole, the international account and resilience of internal production and the capacity of the country had been greatly underestimated. Planning, if that was synonymous with prediction, had been a resounding failure. This flaw of calculus continues. In the following pages, a brief review of eighth plans is given.

The First Five Year Plan was launched in 1951. It laid the foundation of development in agriculture, irrigation, community development, transport and communication. It provided for rehabilitation of refugees, provided a base for growth by improving land and tenure system. It aimed to revive the village, cottage and small-scale industries and prepared the ground for industrialisation. It laid down physical targets of production, in agriculture, particularly food grains, cotton and jute and in industrial the committed resources of Rs. 2,374 crore, the actual outlay came to Rs. 1,968 crore only.

The Plan was too small to be effective, particularly in industry. According to the late T.T. Krishnamachari, it was a plan of preparation and it was successful to a large measure.

It aimed at substantially increasing industrialisation, employment and national income and at reducing inequality of income and wealth. It laid great emphasis on public investment and rapid industrialisation. The basic pattern of investment was shifted from agriculture to industry, while in the industrial sector emphasis was laid on capital-intensive heavy industries, particularly steel. It envisaged setting up of three steel plants in the public sector, extension of two private sector plants, 75 per cent rise in coal production, cement production and extensive development of railway infrastructure.

It envisaged an investment of Rs. 6,200 crore of which Rs, 3,800 crore was to be in the public sector and

Rs. 2,400 crore in the private sector and Rs. 2,400 in the private sector along with a current development of Rs. 1,000 crore. The Second Plan sought to create employment for about 80 lakh persons and it sought to open up new frontiers to build up a sound edifice of infrastructure and to promote industrialization involving capital-intensive projects.

Its programmes may be judged by the fact that the net national income rose by 20 per cent against a target of 25 per cent and per capita income rose by 8 per cent against a target of 18 per cent. The shortfall was due to the annual population growth at the rate of 2.2 per cent against an estimate of 1.2 per cent. The per capita consumption of basic necessities like food, clothing and shelter remained much below the target. It therefore, failed to improve the standard of living.

Exports during the Plan were Rs. 2,965 crore. There was a rise of 3.3 per cent in exports. The target in imports was Rs. 4,350 crore, but imports rose to Rs. 5,402 crore, recording a rise of 24.5 per cent. The balance of payments was adverse by Rs. 2,339 crore. A more disquiting feature was the steep rise of 30 per cent in prices and it could not create adequate additional opportunities for employment.

The Plan shifted the basic emphasis from agriculture to industry rather too soon with consequent failures in food grains, commercial crops. Price stability and exchange surplus. But it promoted the public sector for industrialization and resource mobilisation. It promoted infrastructural development in energy, transport, etc. and provided a foundation for accelerated economic growth.

The Third Plan (1961-66) was framed when there were crises on the financial, foreign exchange, and food fronts. Experts were critical of India's overambitious plan which laid emphasis on welfare at the expense of efficiency and at reduction of inequalities at the cost of raped economic development. This plan aimed at an annual increase of over 5 per cent in national income, self-sufficiency in food grains, expansion of basic industries like steel, chemicals, fuel and power, promoting industrialization and increasing employment. It sought to achieve a 5.4 per cent annual increase in national income and 3.2 per cent annual increase in per capita income.

The Plan envisaged a public sector investment of Rs. 6,300 crore, while investment in the private sector was to be Rs. 4,100 crore. The total outlay was thus Rs. 10,400 crores. The actual expenditure in the public sector was, however, Rs. 8,576.5 crore. The strategy was to expand the infrastructure in the energy, transport and communication sectors.

During the Plan period, inflationary pressure increased in the economy. There was a big rise in non-plan expenditure and deficit financing. During that Plan period, there was floods and droughts, wars with China and Pakistan, increase in defence expenditure and delays and uncertainties in external aid. The Plan failed to generate employment and there was stagnation in the absorption of surplus labour. There was an increase in the concentration of wealth. In the five years, prices rose by 36 per cent. The balance of payments crisis became deep, leading to a partial devaluation of the rupee.

There were three annual plans for the years 1966-67, 1967-68 and 1968-69 respectively. The annual plans were to prepare ground for the fourth Plan. Our agricultural strategy producing new high yield seeds etc., was laid in the Annual Plans and there was exploitation of irrigation potential.

The Fourth Five Year Plan (1969-74) envisaged an

aggregate outlay of Rs. 24,882 crore of which Rs. 15,902 crore was assigned to the public sector. Unfortunately, there were shortfalls in achievements of the various targets laid down. There were failures in the energy and transport sectors. Inflation increased very much and unemployment rose and there was poplation explosion.

The Fifth Plan (1974-79) envisaged an outlay of Rs. 39,303 crore for the public sector and Rs. 27,050 crore for the private sector. In view of the Fourth Plan experience and galloping inflation, the Fifth Plan lowered the target growth rate to 4.4 per cent even compared to the darft Plan which envisaged a growth rate of 5.5 per cent Even the reduced targets were not achieved. about 25 million people were without employment. There was no self-sufficiency in financial resources and foreign debt increased.

The sixth Plan (1980-85) tried to raise the national income, modernise technology, reduce poverty and unemployment, develop the energy sector, improve th standard of living of the masses and reduce inequalities in income and wealth. It was to promote balanced regional development and control population through Family Planning and ecological improvement. The development strategy was to make a material contribution to remove poverty and to achieve full employment over a period of fifteen years. An annual growth rate of 5.2 per cent in per capita income was also contemplated.

The total plan investment was estimated at Rs. 1,58,710 crore of which Rs. 84,000 crore (53 per cent) was to be in the public sector and Rs. 74,710 crore (47 per cent) in the private sector. A total outlay of Rs. 1,72,210 crore was envisaged for the Sixth Plan. The public sector outlay was estimated at Rs. 74,100 crore. The resource mobilizations was to be through public savings, private savings, domestic savings and inflow from abroad. Furing the Plan period the balance of trade deficit had increased from Rs. 2,370 crore in 1979-80 to Rs. 3,970 crore in 1984-85. The balance of payments deficit was Rs. 9,053 crore.

The Seventh Plan was to consolidate the gains of past investment spread over three and a half decades of Indian planning and to take the country on the path of further development leading to equality and a tangible rise in social consumption and welfare. It was to remove poverty, promote, self-reliance through expert promotion and import substitution and import substitution. It was to promote efficiency in organisation. Resource mobilisation through public sector at 1984-85 prices was the to the extent of Rs. 1,80,000 crore. It envisaged a total investment of Rs. 3,22,366 crore, 40 per cent of which was to be financed from domestic sources, calling for tremendous effort at resource mobilization. The Plan sought to bring about a massive shift in favour of the poor. According to the mid-term appraisal available, for the Seventh Plan, the growth rate was 5 per cent, but the 1986-87 realisation was 4 per cent.

The Eighth Plan's clear-cut priorities were to expand employment, squeeze inflation and rein in the deficit in the country's account. Hence, the VIII Plan with employment as its central objective was different from the earlier Plans which had considered employment as a by-product of growth. The earlier plans were mainly related to the allocation of scarce domestic and foreign resources in various sectors. The Seventh Plan had projected a decline in poverty line to 29 per cent by 1988-89 but its level was 39 per cent in 1988.

In the VIII Plan, investment in small-scale industries was increased to give more direct employment. The basic objectives of theVIII Plan are:

— Revenue deficits of the Centre and the States should be reduced to nil by 31 march, 1995.

— The fiscal resources should be equally distributed.

— There should be fiscal discipline.

Further, revenue budget, both plan and non-plan should be considered as a whole. The monetary and fiscal policies should be effectively implemented to control excessive money creation. The mounting revenue expenditure which had grown at rate of 18.7 per cent during 1981-87 must be reduced. But these objectives remained only good intentions and nothing much was achieved. It, of course, had laid emphasis on human development and people's participation as had been the case in earlier plans as well.

The VIII Plan reflected the ideas of the government of the day. there were thus essential contradictions between planning as part of a long-term perspective and democratic elections as a result of which new government might come every five years. Thus, if different governments brought their new plan the whole concept of continuous long-term planning could be in jeopardy. Planning should, in fact, be a matter of national consensus and above political party lines. Planning sould not be an excercise in populism.

Targets envisaged under the Ninth Plan document are not difficult to be achieved at all. However, in order to achieve the target of 230 million tonnes of food production by the end of the Plan period, formulation of a perspective plan for five years indicating targets cropwise, seasonwise, yearwise and areawise taking into consideration the production potential at current technological level on one hand and annual action plan focusing the strategic planning for achieving the targets on the other, is absolutely essential. The annual action plan should include detailed estimates of required inputs, viz high yielding varietal seeds or hybrid seeds, okrganic manure and chemical fertilizers, farm machinery and equipment, irrigation, pesticides and post—harvest facilities areawise. Besides, sources of their availability from various agencies, viz private, co—operative and government sectors should be indicated so as to make them available on time. Transfer of technology through field level trained extension staff as well as mass media will have to be ensured. In fact, past experience has very well confirmed and established that our extension services at field level has been inefficient which should be made most responsive to the present needs. A modified system from thelesson learnt on "Training and Visit System" to suit different agro—ecological regions and social system may be necessary.

The State level corporations and boards, viz Electricity Boards, Seed Corporation, Ground Water Development Corporation, Agro—Industries Corporations, Soil Testing Laboratories, Krishi Vigyan Kendras, Marketing Boards/Federations, Co–operative organizations and the like primarily responsible to play the vital and catalytic role in the promotion and growth of food grain production in particular and other farm commodities in general should also be made to respond and commit themselves for showing the expected results rather than detailing excuses. Input delivery and marketing system which involve the above agencies needs to be revamped without any delay.

In order to reduce the cost of production per unit quantity and increase productivity, production and profitability of the food grain production, there is an urgent need to ensure the folowing:

— The seed industry both n public and private sectors should not only produce quality seeds of food crops but also guide farmers in respect of time, method of sowing and amount of seeds to be used along with agronomic practices to be adopted for optimum productions.

— The fertilizer industry should arrange for soil testing and advising farmers on the time and method of application and amount of chemical fertilizers along with manure to be used for specific food crops.

— The pesticide industry should educate farmers on integrated pest management in respect of food crops concerned.

— The authorities concerned with the supply of canal or ground water should counsel farmers on a continuing basis about the time and method of application of water as also quantum of water to be applied so as to optimize the use of water for specific food crops.

— The suppliers of farm implements and machineries must advise users for specified types of farm operations to be conducted as per schedule which can minimize the cost of okperations. It is high time that these agencies are not only directed to supply quality inputs on time at reasonable rates but also provide full extension support to growers. They should be held responsible for poor quality, late deleivery, high rates and inefficient extension services which have adversely affected soil helath, crop health and production.

Post—harvest facilities have been found grossly inadequate in almost all the States. They should be properly installed particularly in respect of preservation, transport, processing and storage at consumer level.

Research in all aspects should be a continuing process which calls for alloccaton of substantial financial resources, equipment, laboratories and trained manpower. Endeavour should be made to allocate at least one per cent of the Gross Domestic Product (GDP) as against hardly 0.3 per cent today. Besides, the private sector as also the financil institutions should be encouraged to contribute funds to this area in one or the other form. Duplication of research work should be avoided and targets for research results should be considered necessary. At the university level, effective integration among research, extention and educational wings should be established in order to create the desired impact at field level.

Biogas plants already installed and lying out of order throughout the country should immediately be activated through Panchayati Raj or private sector effort inorder to make available enriched organic manure to the fields which have been showing soil–sickness. Similarly, an intensive drive for popularizing compost–making at the farm level and adoption of green manuring and biofertilizers by the farmers should be launched. This will alone help restore soil productivity and mend the damage done by chemical fertilizers.

All the districts, if not the blocks besides the Krishi Vigyan Kendras should have facilities of soil and water testing. However,l all blocks should have well–organized and efficient input delivery system.

Though continuous and heavy dose of subsidy is not desirable, production, procurement and distribution of food grains may have to be subsidised inview of:

— these being items of daily requirement by one and all;

— their productivity and profitability per unit area and time cannot be ckmpared with cash crops; and

— a slight increase in their cost of production would trigger off chain reactions on Indian economy. Thus, all–out steps including a strong political will may be necessary to reduce their cost of production and ensure that farmers do not lose interest incultivating them. Besides, a viable framework for subsidizing food grain production, procurement and distribution may have to be evolved.

As cost of production varies considerably among different agro–ecological zones as well as food grains raised by canal water and through use of diesel engines and wlectric pumpsets, the procurement price should be based taking into consideration these variances.

The approach and attitude of the bank personnel towards financing food grain prodction should be in tune with the changing socio–economic necessity. Not only procedures of lending need to be simplified but adequate autonomy also should be given to banks in respect of deciding the scale of financ, margin, security, rate of interest, model of financing, etc rather than imposing everything on them. The National Bank for Agriculture and Rural Development (NABARD) has done yeoman service in preparing the potential linked plan for the districts indicating yearwise targets for the Ninth Plan period which should be achieved in close co—ordination with village and block Panchayati raj institutions.

Planning and implementation of the annual action plan should be developed over to village and block PRIs and its achievements be reviewed and monitored by the District PRI. Needed infrastructural support along with extension services should be properly identified and appropriately planned in advance to be provided by the State government on time.

Technology is the "in" thing for elite circles in

industry as well as in agriculture for operational policies to be determined. This has implications—economic, social and political—which should not be missed in the wider context of the course and content of the entire economic and social development process.

There is, first of all, a high cost financing improvements in production and productivity of viable farmers and the marketing of surpluses from may be generated in the farm sector. The gains in agriculture too are monopolized in their entirety by the rich and party middle farmers who constitute hardly ten per cent of the farming population. The so-called incentive prices, guaranteed for the marketable surpluses, which under the system of public procurement have been scaled up even as production and productivity have risen, have distorted the structure of relative prices within agriculture and as between agriculture and non-agricultural sectors. Surpluses for investment in industry and for relief to the vulnerable sections of society, especially those which have no viable assets in land, have consequently eroded and processes of balanced economic and social growth have been blocked instead of receiving a boost from agricultural growth in the last three decades.

It is interesting to note in this context the new ambitions which the beneficiaries of the new agricultural strategy have been nursing and have now acquired a critical importance after the structural adjustment based on market-oriented liberalization-globalization process was initiated in 1991. Important in this context too is the proposition which began to be advanced in influential quarters in the late half of the seventies that the "export principle" should apply as much to agriculture as to industry; more so to agriculture in which in recent years surpluses to effective demand in the domestic market have begun to appear from time to time and are creating their own set of problems. This is an extension of the demand for the so-called principle of "parity of prices" between what the surplus farmer sells in the Indian market and what he buys. The idea is that price determination for agricultural produce should be governed relative to the highest price which can be fetched in the global market and not by any reference to a system or structure of relative prices of goods or labour (that is, wages) in the domestic market. There is, of course, at the same time a demand for protection against competitive prices. A logical further extension of this reasoning necessarily is that it is right economically to export agricultural surpluses rather than use them for satisfaction of the needs of those in the country who for want of adequate purchasing power are unable to provide a profitable market for increases in production. The commercial principle, after all, has a logic of its own had if applied to agricultural surpluses it must grant precedence to profit of the surplus producer rather than to the satisfaction of human wants.

Of special interest in this context again is the agriculture versus industry debate which began forcefully to be raised as commercial agriculture made headway. It is suggested by the votaries of higher priority for agriculture that India's development programmes and plans have been a failure because more resources have been pumped into industry, specially heavy industry, during the planning era and agriculture has been starved of funds and investment. It is argued that this resource allocation pattern should change and agriculture should have higher share in total financial outlays in development plans. It is, however, a distortion of reality to say, since after the launching of the new agricultural strategy in the mid-sixties, that agricultural development has suffered on account of greater priority for industry in the economic development process. The resource stringency has, on the contrary, been a far bigger constraint on industrial investment. The worst hit, of course, has been the social services sector. So far as the agricultural sector is concerned, the diversion of resources in favour of commercial farming has been considerable and impressive.

It is not at all enlightening to examine the allocation of resources in terms only of the budgetary allocations in the plans. There have been crash programmes for agricultural production outside the framework of the plans with their accent on additional non-Plan allocations. Thought the commercial banks have been oriented towards providing working capital needs of industry, agriculture began to claim a sizeable share in bank credit also. But the most important change has been a shift in the terms of trade in favour of agricultural sector through the policy of "incentive" procurement prices, especially of food grains. The huge income derived by surplus farmers on this account have been supplemented during the years of comparative shortages by black market prices extracted by the rich farmers in collusion with traders. The higher incomes originating in the agricultural sector have, moreover, been tax-free. The surplus farmers have been getting, in addition to subsidized supplies of various inputs, like irrigation, power and fertilizers. The huge public investment in irrigation, power and fertilizers, therefore, does not give returns and has been showing big losses so that resources for additional investment on infrastructural facilities for the development of the agricultural as well as the industrial sector has had to be drawn from other than those who benefit from these subsidies.

It is indiputable, opf course, that strains in the economy cannot be relieved unlwss indian agriculture is able to produce adequate surpluses. The question, however, is whether it is at all possible to achieve this objective merely by budgetary allocation at the cost of further decay in social services and stagnation in industrial investment. The fact is that any scheme for the development of agriculture and uplift of the rural economy qas a whole cannot become viable and will not be possible to sustain unless industry and more specifically heavy industry grows at a rate faster than that of other segments of the economy,l including agriculture. This is borne out by elaborate input—output calculations and exercises in material balances and linkages that are involved in the growth process.

It was in the very initial stages of framing an economic development strategy in India that he question of the relative weight and pace of the development of heavy industry in relation to wage goods production, especially in the agricultural sector, was closely examined. A galaxy of internationally renowed economists who assisted aIndian planners in drawing up the I and the II Five Year Plans during the fifties was unamious that heavy industry would have to be developed at a rate taster than the overall rate of development of the national economy.

By simple calcuations with respect to material balances in a developing Indian economy, it was established that the desired rates of agricultural output and consumer goods production would require import of machinery and equipment on a scale which would be difficult to finance. The development of an indigenous heavy industry to meet this requirements was, therefore forced by the course of development of the Indian economy in the last three decades, particularly in respect of developments in the agricultural sector.

Growth rate

This is a materialistic age, even in India. The old Charvaka dictum of high consumption based on borrowing seems to be the central philosophy of Indian polilcy—makers. "Borrow and drink ghee," advised Charvaka, "as long as you live, enjoy yourself." While this may not be a bad philosophy for an individual, it can be disastrous for a nation as many Latin Americal countries found out in the 1980s. The consequences of living beyond one's means are reaped by nations much sooner than anticipated by policy—makers.

Materialism is a new religion and a new fundamentalism. What has given rise to it called "growth". The Indian economy grew at 5.5 per cent per annum in the second half of the 1980s. There were few countries in the world which had a higher growth rate than India during the 1980s. Yet economist Jagdish Bhagwati called India's growth performance 'dismal'.

The Ninth Plan is targeting a rate of growth of seven per cent. A high rate of growth at any cost, seems to be the sole objective. It is important to ask if a high rate of growth necessarily implies that the economy is in a better shape.

Growth is a superficial phenomenon. We must look below the surface to see if the country can sustain the growth. The Latin Americal countries grew at 5.3 per cent annually between 1973—80. Then came the debt crisis and growth rates became negative. The Indian economy grew at over 5 per cent during the 1980s while external debt increased from about $ 20 billion during the decade. The high rate of growth of the 1980s has been hailed as the result of partial liberalization by the Finance Secretary Montek S. Ahluwalia. Critics have, therefore, blamed the limited import liberalization in the 1980s for the crisis of the early 1990s. Both views may be correct. Boom and the crisis were inseparable because of the nature of growth. The higher growth of the domestic economy, agreed Bimal Jalan of the Planning Commission, was financed by external loans on hard terms... 'this has proved to be a mistake'.

The question is how many times should we make the same mistake? Given our economic situation and the fiscal position, high growth targets can become a major destabilizing influence. The rate of saving which is the most important factor influencing growth continues to remain stagnant for the last few years. The slight increase in the rate witnessed a year ago, may not be sustained if one goes by financial savings indicators. India wants to grow as fast as the East Asian economies. But without a policy–frame to raise the rate of saving and sustain it at the higher rate, it would be impossible to maintain a high rate of growth without periodic crises. The policy frame, however, appears to be working in the opposite direction. Liberalization of gold imports, withdrawal of incentives on savings, consumerism and huge revenue account deficits are not conducive to higher savings.

The strategy in the post—libealization period has been to rely on foreign capital to maintain the high rates of growth of the eighties. If in the eighties, the growth was fuelled by external borrowings, in the nineties it should be fulled by foreign investments. This is what our present policy is. Foreign investment is the most sought after commodity today. Politicians and bureaucrats are now busy "selling" India to the foreign investor. Non—debt capital inflows to developing countries have increased tremendously in recent years. And, therefore, it may be possible for India to attract foreign portfolio and direct investments to a certain extent. Portfolio investments can, of course, be volatile and therefore an extremely risky source of investment finance. Hence, the stress is on attracting foreign direct investment. And, it is here that India is not succeeding to the extent that is needed to sustain high rates of growth. It is probable that foreign direct investment will not come in large amounts into India as the country continues to have a current account deficit and high indebtedness. The foreign investor sees substantial transfer and political risks in investing in India.

Where this development strategy which relies on inflow of foreign capital (instead of external debts as in the eighties) to sustain high growth rates, is a desirable policy is an important question. But even if we accept its desirability, it is not a feasible strategy as foreign direct investments will not make good the shortfalls in resources needed for sustaining a seven per cent rate of growth.

The update to the Economic Survey 1995—96, published about seven months ago, had emphasised three key challenges for economic policy: how to control the fiscal deficit; how to provide adequate and reliable economic infrastructure services at a reasonable cost and with sustainable financing and pricing policies; and how to ensure broad—based employment–generating growth of agriculture, industry and other sectors, together with strengthened programmes for basic social services and anti—poverty programmes to ensure a rapid alleviation of poverty.

These challenges remain central to our concerns. It is essential to keep reducing the Centre's fiscal deficit to below four per cent of GDP as soon as possible in order to: reduce interest rates and free up resources to finance the high levels of investment, both public and private, envisaged in the Approach Paper to the Ninth Plan; to contain Central Government borrowing from the RBI and thus check the growth of inflationary potential and pressures; to moderate the growth of rapidly rising interest payments which preempt the resources available for spending on priority, social and infrastructure needs; to facilitate orderly development of the market for long—term debt securities which is so essential for fostering the financing of infrastructure: and to reduce the risks associated with excessive government borrowing from external sources.

The path of fiscal deficit reduction is well known in teory as it is difficult to implement in practice. We must preserve with our programme of tax reforms which has helped to raise the ratio of revenues to GDP. We must seek higher non—tax revenues in the form of larger dividends from Government equity in public enterprises. We must reduce the growth of subsidies through better targeting and much more systematic application of user charges for Government services. The normally difficult task of expenditure management will be accentuated in the coming years by the challenge of accommodatingthe recommendations of the Fifth Central Pay Commission. Finally Government must act expeditiously on the recommendations of the Disinvestment Commission.

The responsibility for fiscal consolidation and prudence does not rest with the Central Government alone. The States have to do their part in reducing their borrowing requirements through better design and implementation of their tax systems and through steps to curb low priority expenditures.

The recurring power failures even in the capital city of Delhi this winter underline the critical nature of the power problem throughout the country. Because of unavailable, uncertain or erratic supplies from the public grid, the economy is paying a heavy price in the form of foregone production, lost exports of goods and services, frustrated investment intentions, recourse to high cost captive power generation, loss of international competitiveness, and barriers to the spread of information technology which is redefininf the terms of production, technical progress and international specialisation thhroughout the world. The key elements of the Commonm Minimum National Action Plan for Power, which need to be pursued vigorously, include the establishment of independent State Electricity Regulatory Commissions, the rationalisation of retail power tariffs, induction of private participation in electricity distribution and the restructuring and corporatisation of State Electricity Boards to run on commercial principles.

Power is only one, albeit critical, component of our energy economy. Today, the development of our petroleum sector is under a serious threat, with crude oil production having declined, oil imports rising sharply and the deficit on the Oil Pool Account rising each day and expected to exceed Rs. 15,000 crore before the end of this financial year. There is no economically viable alternative to adjusting petroleum prices to reflect the impact of international oil price increases. Furthermore, if we are to reap the benefits of increased investment and efficient production in all stages of the petroleum sector (ranging from exploration and development to refining and distribution), We must carry out a phased dismantling of the existing administered price mechanism in this sector. The time for initiating this reform is already overdue.

A pick—up in the growth momentum of the economy will intensify the need for gerneing increasing amounts of foreign savings to meet the investment requirements of economy and to sustain the growth momentum itself. Foreign direct investment flows provide such savings without adding to the country's external debt. As indicated in the Common Mnimum Programme, foreign direct investment should rise to US $

10 billion per year from the current level of US $ 2 to 3 billion. We must learn from the pragmatic nationalism of China which received around US $ 40 billion of investment in 1996, and expects to attract more in 1997. We must also learn from the flexibility and speed of Indonesia, which modified its policies rapidly in response to perceived competition from China and India, to double foreign investment inflows between 1994 and 1995. We must ensure that the regulations governing the inflow of foreign investment are transparent and attractive in comparison with what other Asian economies offer. A review of FERA is underway in this context.

Fifty years after achieving independence, poverty, illiteracy, disease and lack of minimum social services continue to afflict hundreds of millions of our afflict hundreds of millions of our people. Experience from all over the world shows that rapid all over the world shows shows that rapid, employment—generating growth is the most effective way of reducing poverty. Our policies and programmes must accord the highest priority to encouraging growth of sustainable and productive job opportunities in all sectors. In agriculture, income earning opportunities for farmers should be expanded by removing existing impediments to domestic and international trade in agricultural products and removing controls on key agro-processing industries. At the same time, there have to be renewed efforts to strengthen rural infrastructure in the form of irrigation, rural roads, soil conservation, seed development, research and extension, and rural credit systems. In many cases this may call for a review and redirection of existing programmes. Besides, it is imperative to find incrmental resources for public investment in rural infrastructure. Such resources can be raised only partly through the budget. Without hurting the poor, the bulk of the resources would from the larger and better—off farmers.

There is a tremendous scope for expanding productive employment in the construction and other service sectors, especially in the cities and towns. But torealise this potential, the Government must be prepared to remove impediments imposed by various laws and regulations, such as the Urban Land Ceiling Act.

For the vast majority of our people to benefit from extension of job opportunities stemming from rapid labour—intensive grwoth, there has to be acommensurate expansion and quality improvement in the basic social services such as primary eduction and primary health care. The experience of countries as diverse as China and Indonesia has demosntrated the critical requirement for priority attention to these basic services.

For those at the margins of a market driven economy the effective provison of minimum social services and special programmes, for employment and poverty alleviation fulfill an essential need. Over time these special programmes have proliferated, not always rationally. The maximise the beneficial impact of anti—poverty programmes, it would be desirable to seek ways of consolidation and rationalisation, and some attrition. The basic goal should be to enhance sustainable benefits to the poorest segments of the society, while reducing administrative duplication and wastage and minimising well—known "leakages."

Over the last 5 to 6 years the Indian economy has demonstrated enviable resilience and buoyancy as a result of wide ranging economic reforms and closer integration with the world economy. On the whole, those dimension of the economy have performed best where reform efforts have been most thorough and far reaching. We must learn from this experience as we look ahead to meet the challenges of the future.

Whether it is fully realized or not, the Ninth Plan

planning represents a new age planning of an age of management culture, economic restructuring, resource scarcity, economy, value for investment, global competition, MNCs, mega investments, free trade, intellectual property rights, R & D, productivity, quality, efficiency, hardware and software of production, human capital, strategic planning, economic vision, government-private sector partnership, value by results, international capital, regional economic groupings, delicensing, decentralization, lean taxation, FDI, foreign borrowings, JVs, market pricing, opening of the economies, public-private sector parity or equality, fiscal discipline, public-orientation, deregulations, budgetary imbalances, de-nationalisation, corporate takeovers, subsidy-cuts, commercialization of agriculture and free trade in agricultural goods, non-farm enterprises in rural areas, entrepreneurship, innovations, paid lunches, cutting down free rides, user-charges, gender equality and empowerment of women, and soon.

In spite of its not insignificant achievements, the bane of Indian planning has been poor implementation and results, viz operational shortcomings and 'targetism'. The Ninth Plan should and ought to make a break from it, to justify its nearly Rs. 1 m crore investment. It must have multiple effect, without which it is bad planning, though the plans do not work out the multipliers. The plan has to learn a leaf or two from corporate planning, particularly of MNCs which mean business of every dollar of investment. Not that the Plan should be devoid of human concerns and values, which it or for that matter any public planning anywhere should be responsive to, given the concern of planning with the have-nots. That is, the results of the planning need be measured not only, by the hard facts of growth rate but also by the light and laughter in the lives of the common people, visible to the naked eye. Otherwise, the purpose of the whole planning exercise would be much lost. All said and done, the fact should be brought home to the planners in the Ninth Plan that it requires a lot of suffering and sacrifice to make the Plan operative with so much investment and it should yield commensurate returns in health, education, employment, social infrastructure, economic overheads, employment, enterprises, etc. for which the Plan is intended. India is one of the most poverty-ridden and low income countries. Our per capita income is not even $ 400 per annum. Millions and millions of people's daily concerns water, sanitation, medical aid, food and employment. Accordingly, the new age planning consists of making plan investments go as far as possible or maximum yielding. Planning must make the deserts bloom, not allow the forests to vanish so to say. If not, it is not proper planning.

Whether the plan size is optimal, suboptimal or overoptimal is irrelevant in the context of the plan. From plan-to-plan, planning efforts anyhow need to be raised. Considering This the plan is not at all oversized, considering the magnitude of the problems facing the economy and the efforts needed to overcome them. It is a different thing if the nation opts for a soft and small Ninth Plan. At no time, the plans had escaped the label of being ambitious and oversized. Notwithstanding plan size, the basic economic problems remain intact, if the poverty-line population increasing recently to 37 per cent is any indication.

Only, the Ninth Plan should be a new age planning or plan of operational efficiency, economy, efficiency, discipline, human and grass roots development, competitive, forward looking, co-ordinating and comprehensive. In addition, it must be time and cost bound. No doubt, it is a tall order of things but it is unavoidable if the Ninth Plan is to spell a success and make a dent into the thousand problems of the economy and the people. We have been lethargic with planning and it is time to be strictly business and management minded about planning and plan and the Ninth Plan is the right and opportune time to commence new age planning, without which it becomes increasingly difficult to sustain planning.

That is the law of diminishing returns which appears to have set in planning, since long, needs to be reversed in the Ninth Plan, failing which zero and even negative marginal productivities may set in for plan investments. There are increasing constraints on plan resources due to which the Ninth Plan should successfully go through its arithmetic of investments and returns in different lines of production and try to realize them for the first time in planning history of the country in tune with the new age stress on returns rather than or just investments. The Ninth Plan, in other words, should incorporate into its functioning strict business principles. The Plan thus should open a new chapter in planning not only in India but also the world over. Planning should assert itself and march ahead in the so-called market ruled economy and dispense its benefits to its large multitudes standing second to none in economy, efficiency and execution. It is the mandate of the populace. There is a national consensus behind planning, particularly the Ninth Plan, which promises to be a plan of action and of the people. It promises to give thrust to the thrust areas. Economy, productivity, returns and people should be the watchwords of new planning to commence with the Ninth Plan. There is no activity commensurate in importance with the Plan that should be No. 1 programmes, as nothing involves such a massive investment and the welfare and happiness of millions and millions of people and their living and natural environment.

One has to harp at length about the need for new planning because of the debris that is being left behind by improper planning, which is downward rather than upward. Rural development, for instance, is a greatly neglected aspect of our planning and the Ninth Plan promises to remove the whole backlog of it including human resource development and women and child development. Great challenges lay ahead of the new planning process.

The Government was not content with mere re-establishment of law and order. It was keen that the new sense of national purpose should be harnessed to a speedier promotion of economic growth and social justice. On 1 July, 1975, the Prime Minister announced in a nationwide broadcast a "Twenty-Point Economic Programme" designed to achieve speedy development and to remove many of the evil practices which and persisted all these years, including bonded labour and rural indebtedness. It gave a further fillip to the official drive to contain inflation and root out black money. The programme was acclaimed by all sections of the people notably farmers and landless workers, industrial workers, representatives of trade and industry, and students and teachers. This meant:

— Continuance of steps to bring down prices of essential commodities. Streamlined production, procurement and distribution of essential commodities. Strict economy in government expenditure.

— Implementation of agricultural land ceilings and speedier distribution of surplus land compilation of land records.

— Stepping up of provision of house sites for landless and weaker sections.

— Bonded labour, wherever it exists, will be declared illegal.

— Plan for liquidation of rural indebtedness. Legislation for moratorium on recovery of debt from landless labourers, small farmers and artisans.

— Review of laws on minimum agricultural wages.

— Five million more hectares to be brought under irrigation. National programme for use of underground water.

— An accelerated power programme. Super thermal stations under central control.

— New development plan for development of handloom sector.

— Improvement in quality and supply of people's cloth.

— Socialisation of urban and urbanisable land. Ceiling on ownership and possession of vacant land and on plinth area of new dwelling units.

— Special squads for valuation of conspicuous construction and prevention of tax evasion. Summary trails and deterrent punishment of economic offenders.

— Special legislation for cónfiscation of smugglers' properties.

— Liberalisation of investment procedures. Action against misuse of import licences.

— New schemes for workers' association of industry.

— National permit schemes for road transport.

— Income Tax relief to middle class; exemption limit placed at Rs. 8,000.

— Essential commodities at controlled prices to students in hostels.

— Books and stationery at contolled prices.

— New apprenticeship scheme to enlarge employment and training, especially of weaker sections.

Involvement of all the 860 institutions and agencies of the Indian Council of Agricultural Research (ICAR), agricultural universities and voluntary agencies for the transfer of farm techniques to the field level with adoption of 50,000 agricultural families in the programme, has been recommended by the ICAE national workshop on transfer of technology programme for rural development.

The three-day workshop has also decided to prepare a "lab to land operational manual" providing information on all available technologies, besides embarking upon a continuous monitoring and evaluation of the implementation of the programme for making midcourse corrections. Such a manual will pay special attention to the small and marginal farmers and provide viable technology to them.

The workshop has decided that while ICAR and its agencies and the agricultural universities and their centres should adopt 20,000 farmers each, the voluntary organisations and affiliated agricultural college could be entrusted with the task of adopting 10,000 families.

The workshop felt that in selecting centres, preference should be given to institutions already involved in agricultural development and the selection of blocks, villages, farm families should also be preferably from the intensive agricultural development blocks already identified.

The approach for the transfer of technology should be on a cluster-village basis and proximity of the implementing agency should also be borne in mind for effective supervision.

Another important recommendation of the workshop was that related programmes for farm youth, farm women and children should be taken up simultaneously. It also strongly recommended creation of suitable marketing infrastructure and facilities well in advance to match the anticipated increased production.

The workshop recommended organisation of agricultural exhibitions at national, State, institute and university levels, during the national extension fortnight celebrations—inter—State and inter-regional exchanges, lectures by farm-professors organisation of debates and discussions special programmes and features on the radio, television, press and extension lectures should be taken up during the fortnight, it said.

Rural development planning in India was introdrced in the light of experiments for rural uplift prior to Independence by the Father of the Nation, Mahatma Gandhi in Sevagram, Rabindranath Tagore in villages around Santiniketan, Spencer Hatch in Travancore (erstwhile), V.T. Krishnamachari in Kasamba near Baroda, and F.L. Brayne in Gurgaon in the 1920s and after Independence by Prakasham, Albert Mayer and Horace Holmes, S.K. Dey et al. The first massive rural development endeavour called the Community Development Programme was launched with the beginning of the First Five Year Plan itself. This was a co-operative partnership between the government and the people for the all-round development of the people in a particular area. With the commencement of Panchayati Raj, it had to become the programme for the people, of the people, and by the Third Five Year Plan, the entire country was covered with community development blocks numbering over 5,000. The community development blocks became the units of administration, planning, co-ordination, and development for rural people with the focus on integrated rural development, comprising agriculture and allied activities, rural industries, education, health socail welfare, communications, supplementary employment with special focus on self-help and public partcipation. A schematic budget of Rs. 17 lakh per block—Rs. 12 lakh for stage one (5 years) and Rs. 5 lakh for stage two (another 5 years)—was provided. The staffing patern comprised the Block Development Officer (BDO) 8 Extension Officers (in agriculture, animal husbandry, co-operative, Panchayats, rural industries, engineering, social education, and programmes for women and children), 10 Gram Sevaks, 2 Gram Sevikas, a Programme Assistant, a Storekeeper-cum-Accountant, with some support staff on the ministerial side prescribed for a standard block.

Measures for the poor

The integrated approach to rural development, however, got gradually diluted with the work relating to village industries being handed over to the Khadi and Village Industries Commission (KVIC) and the growing need for self-reliance in food. The greater emphasis on food production resulted in the launching of the Intensive Agriculture Development Programme (IADP) in selected districts followed by the Intensive Agriculture Areas Programme (IAAP), and the High Yield in Varieties Programme (HYVP). By the late sixties, and the early seventies, it was perceived that even though the intensive effort in agriculture had led to the Green Revolution, the benefits of this remained largely confined to the big farmers and areas which were better placed to receive the benefits of high yielding varieties techonlogy. Therefore, the need to take special measures for benefiting the poorer sections of the population and for development of backward and disadvantaged areas was felt. As a result, programmes like Small Farmers and Agricultural Labourers (MFAL), Crash Scheme for Rural Employment,

Pilot Intensive Rural Employment Programme, Food for Work Programme, Drought-Prone Areas and Desert Development Programmes, and the Minimum Needs Programme were launched.

VI Plan—sharper focus: with the launching of the Sixth Plan the attempts at tackling the problems of the deprived sections of the population and geographical areas were further consolidated, rationalized, and expanded. The SFDA and MFAL were replaced by the Integrated Rural Development Programme (IRDP) which was extended to cover the entire country and its scope expanded to all activities in the primary, secondary, and tertiary sectors. Under this programme, income-base criteria for identification of the target group was prescribed and household approach was adopted. The programme also aimed to provide skills through Training of Rural Youth for Self-Employment (TRYSEM) and assets (through a mix of subsidy and credit with the ultimate objective of raising people above the poverty line. A special programme for economic betterment of rural women, popularly known as Development of Women and Children in Rural Areas (DWCRA), was also developed and linked to the self-employment programme (IRDP). The Food for Work Programme was restructured in the form of wage employment programme known as National Rural Employment Programme, the Rural Landless Employment Guarantee Programme (RLEGP) was launched in 1983-84 with the specific objective of providing up to 100 dats of employment per annum to at least one member of each rural landless household. The programmes of the Sixth Plan were continued with a sharper focus and higher outlays during the Seventh and the Eighth Plan periods. The aforesaid wage employment programmes (NREP & ROEGP) were merged into Jawahar Rozgar Yojana (JRY) and Indira Awaas Yojana (IAY)—a component of JRY—

was strengthened both qualitatively and quantitatively. Subsequently, Employment Assurance Scheme (EAS) was introduced for assured employment up to 100 days in the lean agricultural season.

Rural development mey be construed as total all-round socio-economic development of the rural people and not merely the ongoing programmes such as self-emplyment, wage employment, area development, land reforms, etc. A significant step has already been taken to revitalize the Panchhayati Raj institutions with the enactment of the Constitution (Seventy--third Amendment) Act, 1992 so that 'operation by the people and co-operation by the government' becomes a reality. Accordingly, the State goverment mey, by law, endow the Panchayats with such powers and authority as may be necessary to enastitutions of self-government and such law may contain provisions for devolution of powers and responsibilities upon Panchayats at the appropriate level, subject to such conditions as may be specified therein, with respect to the preparation of plans and implmentation of schemes for economic development and social justice as may be entrusted to them including those in relation to matters listed, as follows, in the XI schedule to the Constitution (Article 243G):

— Agriculture including agricultural extension.

— Land improvement, implementation of land reforms, land consolidation, and soil conservation.

— Minor irrigation, water management, and watershed development.

— Animal husbandry, dairying, and poultry.

— Fisheries.

— Social forest produce.

— Minor forest produce.

— Small-scale industries, including food processing industries.
— Khadi, village, and cottage industries.
— Rural housing.
— Drinking water.
— Fuel and fodder.
— Roads, culverts, bridges, ferries, waterways, and other means of communication.
— Rural electrification, including distribution of electricity.
— Non-conventional energy sources.
— Poverty alleviation programmes.
— Education including primary and secondary school.
— Technical training and vocational education.
— Adult and non-formal education.
— Libraries.
— Cultural activities.
— Markets and fairs.
— Health and sanitation, including hospitals, primary health centres, and dispensaries.
— Family welfare.
— Women and child development.
— Social welfare including welfare of the handicapped and mentally retarded.
— Welfare of the weaker sections, and in particular, of the Scheduled Castes and Scheduled Tribes.
— Public distribution system.
— Maintenance of community assets.

Rural growth

Given enough resources with the government, there is no reason why rural development and through it the eradication of rural poverty cannot be achieved during the five year period of the Plan with hundred per cent success. There is need for continued direct State intervention for poverty alleviation. While the programmes for self-employment and supplementary wage employment would continue in the Ninth Plan, these would be redesingned in order to make them more effective as instruments of poverty alleviation. It is necessary that these programmes are integrated with the various sectoral programmes as well as the area development programmes within the umbrella of the Panchayati Raj institutions.

An important change envisaged in the Ninth Plan is to make self-employment programmes more effective through a shift in strategy under Integrated Rural Developnment Programme (IRDP), from an individual benefiviary approach to a group and/or cluster approach would include development of skills of the rural poor through an inbuilt training component, upgradation of technology, establishment of forward and backward linkages, availability of appropriate infrastructure and markekt tie-ups. It is good that the scheme of Training of Rural Youth for Self-Employment (TRYSEM) is now going to be revamped thoroughly in order to improve the employment opportunities of the poor. It is common knowledge that the artisans in rural areas, despite their rich heritage and skills, belong to the poverty group. Therefore, to improve their skills and production capabilities, they would be provided with modern tool kits as well.

A significant aspect of rural growth would be the improvement in the status of rural women. In this context, already the Development of Women and Children in Rural Areas (DWCRA) has been quite a siccess story in empowering women and in improving their economic status, though only in selected States so far. A mechanism for replicating the successful DWCRA groups would be evolved during the NInth Plan, while it would be integrated with IRDP and TRYSEM to provide womens' groups with greater access to financial resources and training. A country wide Employment Assurance Scheme is also intended to be launched during the Ninth Plan so that during the lean agricultural season, some manual work of casual naure may be given.

Rural poverty is largely among the landless and marginal farmers. Therefore, access to land remains a key element of the anti-poverty strategy in rural areas. Ninth Plan has laid down th e following programme of action for land reforms during the plan period:

(1) Detection as well as redistribution of ceiling surputs land;

(2) Upgradation of land records on a regular basis;

(3) Tenancy reforms providing for recording the rights of tenants and share-croppers;

(4) Consolidation of holding;

(5) Preventing alienation of tribal lands;

(6) Providing access on a group basis to the poor on wastelands and common property resources;

(7) Leasing-in and leasing-out of land will be permitted within the ceiling limits; and

(8) Perfernce to women in the distribution of ceiling surplus land and legal provisions for protecting their rights on land.

Seven basic services have been identified for priority attention with an all-out effort for their complete coverage in a time-bound manner. These are safe drinking water, availability of primary health service facilities, universalisation of primary education, provision of public housing assistance to all shelterless poor families, nuturitional spport to children, and such other aspects as already mentiones before. The Panchayati Raj institutions will function as effective institutions for olcal self-government and social justice and implement schemes in social services.

The village and small industries sector (VSI) has rightly been chosen as the focal point for triggering off the growth process. Industries of this sector will be provided sufficient incentives and support to facilitate their growth and employment potential. Quite importantly, foreing investment will not be allowed to displace these industries. Investment limit for such industries has now already been raised by the government in order to enabele them to achieve economies of scale. It is hoped that the items reserved for production in them will continue to remain so. The VSI sector is to meke a dent in the regional disparities in terms of industrial and overall growth all over the country.

With all the sectoral financial and physical targets laid down, any plan cannot be successful unless the strategy to achieve its various targets is quite sound, practical and does not go awry. The approach paper contents that while it is feasible to achieve a seven per cent growth rate on the basis of the existing behavioural paramenters for private savings and investment, regular and significant revision of the pervasive underpricing of irrigation services, electricity, railway passenger fares, postal and telecommunication rates, perroleum and other mineral prices is required so that both the value-added and savings of these sectors improve substantially and are not eroded.

It is important to realize that for the target growth rate of seven per cent, investment would need to be of the order of 28.6 per ment of GDP. And this would have to be achieved despite a drop in the incremental capital-output ratio (ICOR, its decline shows improvement in efficiency) from 4.34 per cent.This, therfore, brings us to the aspect of allocation and optimal use of funds for doing so. It is expected that this cecline in ICOR would be achieved due to economic reforms, elimination of outdated technologies, higher energy and material efficiency in the industrial sector.

It is also imperative to maintain a balance between thg capital-intensive industry and labour-intensive industry to achieve the plan targets.Ancillary industries should take over manufacture of the componets of the industry set-up through the foreign direct investment route. All said and done, there fully aware of the dimension of resource mobilization. Therefore, it is necessary that both the Centre and the States work out programmes in concrete terms to meet the financing requirements of both infrastructure development and poverty alleviation schemes.

8

Promotional Support

Under the plan scheme for "Promotion of Food Processing Industries", the Ministry provides assistance to Government Departments, Government Undertakings/ Organisations, Non-Government Organisations and Industry Associations for organising exhibitions, workshops, seminars, conferences, symposium with the objective of dissemination of information regarding food processing industries, familiarizing the existing and prospective entrepreneurs with modern techniques of production and packaging, development of market and popularization of products,. It also provides assistance for undertaking studies and surveys for assessment of potential for food processing industries on sectoral and regional basis.

The scheme also envisages financial assistance for Entrepreneurial Development Programmes (EDP). During the year 1998-99, following major exhibitions, workshops, seminars, conferences, studies, entrepreneurial development programmes have been sponsored/assisted by this Ministry.

Exhibitions

The Ministry of Food Processing Industries sponsored the international exposition "Agro-Advantage Maharashtra '98" organised by Government of Maharashtra, during

November 6-9, 98 at Mumbai, to attract investment in the food processing sector.

The exposition was a show-window 'for display of the latest technology in the field of agro food sector from all over the world. The Ministry of Food Processing Industries took active part in the exposition. Secretary (FPI) and other senior officers of the Ministry also participated in the convention, which attracted over 800 delegates. On this occasion, definitive interests have been shown by many national and international groups for investment, in food processing projects with investment outlay exceeding Rs.2000 crores. The Government of Maharashtra will be taking follow up action in this regard.

The Ministry sponsored the International Food Convention (IFCON'98) organised by Association of Food Scientists and Technologists (India), at CFTRI, Mysore during November 24-27, 199 8 to bring on a common platform the captains of food industry, research scientists and technologists from universities and premier research institutions and other food professionals to debate and deliberate upon the emerging issues confronting the country in the face of liberalisation and globalisation of market economies. Secretary (FPI) and other senior officers of the Ministry also attended the convention. Secretary (FPI) presided over the inauguration & opening of Food Expo' 98. He also made a presentation on "Globalisation of Indian Food Industry -Problems & Perspective". The event was attended by a large number of national and international scientists and technologists.

The Ministry of Food Processing Industries participated in the exhibition "Agro-Tech' 98" organised by the Confederation of Indian Industry, Northern Region, at Chandigarh from December 2-6, 1998. The exhibition provided opportunities for interaction and transaction of business to visitors including high power delegation from SAARC nations. Secretary (FPI) and other senior officers of the Ministry also attended the exhibition. Secretary (FPI) inaugurated the International Conference on Fruit & Vegetable Processing which was held on December 2, 1998. This Ministry provided financial assistance for the event.

The Bengal Chamber of Commerce & Industry Guwahati Chapter, organised an exhibition and a seminar "Expo-North East' 98" at Guwahati from 515 December, 1998. NERAMAC, a public sector undertaking under the administrative control of this Ministry, participated in the above event on behalf of the Ministry. The Ministry provided financial assistance for holding this exhibition and seminar on food processing.

The Ministry of Food Processing Industries participated in an exhibition on India's Vision for Future and Achievements of the past 50 years, organised at National Stadium, New Delhi from 5-15th August, 1998. A 30 minute audio visual display, highlighting India's achievements in science and technology over the last 50 years was also shown in the Central Hall of the Parliament House on 15th August, 1998 by the Department of Science & Technology.

The Ministry of Food Processing Industries participated in the Industrial Exhibition organised by Indian Industries Association, which is the APEX body of Small Industries in the State of Uttar Pradesh, at Muzaffarnagar from 4-5th October 1998 exhibition was inaugurated by Shri Sompal, Minister of State for Agriculture.

Seminars & workshops

The Ministry assisted the Centre for Processed Food, Bangalore in organising an international seminar on

'Modified Atmosphere Packaging & Controlled Atmosphere Storage, during April 27-28, 1998 at Bangalore.

This Ministry participated in a "workshop on Packaging of Wheat Flours" organised by the Roller Flour Mills Federation of India at New Delhi on June 19, 1998 to help the manufacturers to improve the packaging methods and explore world market for their products. The workshop was inaugurated by Secretary (FPI).

The World Association for Small & Medium Enterprises, New Delhi in collaboration with National Research Development Corporation organised the Asia-China Technology & Economic Cooperation Expo' 98 (SATAX'98) at New Delhi from 27-30 July, 1998 to promote technological trade & economic cooperation between India and other countries in South Asian Region in FPI & other selected industrial sector. Secretary (FPI) delivered a key note address at the convention. The Ministry also provided financial assistance to the event.

A national seminar on Problems of Small & Marginal Farmers in Marketing of Fruits and Vegetables was organised by the Farmers Education & Welfare Society at New Delhi on the 20th & 21st August 1998. The Ministry provided assistance for holding of this seminar.

The Ministry sponsored a national conference on " The Future of Processed Fruit And Vegetable Industry - Summit '98" hosted by the India Export & Economic Foundation in coordination with All India Food Preservers' Association at Bangalore on August 21-22, 1998. The objective of the conference was dissemination of information amongst the exporters, entrepreneurs, consultants, technologists, statutory authorities and policy makers to build a strong interface between agriculture and industry and to highlight the problems and prospects of exporting processed fruits and vegetables.

ILSI-INDIA, New Delhi, organised a workshop on Science Based Approaches to Harmonisation of Regulatory Food Quality and Safety Measures in SAARC Region to provide scientific inputs for harmonisation of food regulations within member countries of SAARC. The Workshop was inaugurated by Secretary (FPI).

The Department of Business Economics, University of Delhi organised an industrial seminar on 27 October 1998 to promote the study of food processing industries in India in regard to technology, marketing and supply chains, foreign participation etc.

The Ministry provided assistance to Confederation of Indian Food Trade & Industry, New Delhi to organise "Food Processing Summit '98" on 14th November 1998 at New Delhi on "Challenges of Globalisation, Time for Introspection". The seminar was inaugurated by Secretary (FPI).

A one-day seminar on "Potential of Food Processing Industries in North-East with Special reference to Tripura" was held on 16th November 1998 in Agartala. The seminar was organised by the Government of Tripura at the initiative of this Ministry. It was inaugurated by the Chief Minister of Tripura and was attended by Ministers of the Government of Tripura, Members of Parliament, Secretary (FPI) and other senior officers of this Ministry besides representatives of CFTRI, NERAMAC and a large number of entrepreneurs. The seminar was very useful in highlighting the potential of food processing industries in Tripura. Financial assistance was provided for organisation of the seminar.

ILSI-INDIA and Micro-nutrient Initiative, South

Asian Regional Offices have organised a national conference on 'Micro-nutrient Fortification of Food' at Jaipur from 8-9 Feb. '99 against the background of high incidence of malnutrition in the country particularly resulting from vitamin A, iodine and iron deficiencies.

The conference was attended by experts from India and abroad to discuss important issues relating to micro-nutrient fortification of food and safety, regulatory & educational advocacy aspects of food fortification programme in India.

The National Productivity Council, New Delhi is organised a national seminar on "Quality for Leadership-challenges for Indian Food Industry" during February, 1999. The proposed seminar will be very useful for food processing industries in India. This Ministry sponsored this seminar.

Studies

This Ministry has entrusted the National Research Development Corporation to conduct a preferability study for setting Lip an Integrated coconut processing complex in Andaman & Nicobar Islands at a cost of Rs.5.00 lakhs. This Ministry has taken initiative to develop coconut processing facilities in these Islands.

The Ministry of Food Processing Industries has given, in principle, approval to support APEDA's proposal to undertake a techno-feasibility study on cold chain linkages in three States. This study is being done by ATO-DLO, a research organisation under the Ministry of Agriculture, Government of Netherlands. The techno-feasibility exercise in respective states will evolve a strategy for designing a supply chain grid leading to a pilot project for a few specific commodities for ensuring reduction in post-harvest losses and wastage. The study would be an attempt to strike a balance between supply, distribution, storage and demand. ·The financial implications are being worked out by APEDA.

The Ministry has sponsored a study by the Northeaster Industrial and Technical Consultancy Organisation Ltd. (NEITCO), Guwahati on Integrated Master Plan for food processing industry in the Northeastern region and also the role of NERAMAC in this context. The study would focus on the strategy for developing the food processing sector in the region after taking into account the availability of raw material, existing infrastructure and consumer demand. This will also bring out the role which needs to be played by North-Eastern Regional Agricultural Marketing Corporation Ltd. (NERAMAC).

Entrepreneurial development programme

Uttar Pradesh Consultants Limited, Kanpur will be organising two Entrepreneurial Development Programmes in Food Processing Industries at Pratapgarh and Allahabad on the subject of Aonwla processing and guava processing respectively. This programme will help in generating self-employment/ entrepreneurship in the State. This Ministry is providing financial assistance for the two events.

Haryana-Delhi Industrial Consultancy Limited, New Delhi will conduct an Entrepreneurial Development Programme in food processing industries in March, 1999 to identify the prospective entrepreneurs as well as potential investment opportunities. The programme will help in setting up of small units by the prospective entrepreneurs. This Ministry is providing financial assistance for this purpose.

Promotional interactions

The Ministry participated in the International Green

Week Fair (IGW) 1998 held in Germany in the month of January 1998. The IGW Fair is a major consumer fair of Europe for food products and is held every year in Germany for the last six decades. The Ministry's participation this time was at a scale larger than that of the previous year, with Agricultural Products Export Development Authority (APEDA) in association with this Ministry having put up a stall for 'all the 10 days of the fair.

A representative of the Ministry participated as a member in the Promotion Mission led by a senior officer of the Ministry of Industry, Department of Industrial Policy & Promotion, which visited France from 20th to 26th September, 1998. This was In connection with a one day event called "Indo-French Investment Forum" being organised by that Ministry in New Delhi to make a sectoral representation to some of the French medium-sized companies followed by one-to-one meetings. Food processing including packaging is one of the thrust areas selected for the event.

Indo-Italian Joint Working Group on Food Processing was constituted in 1998 by the Ministry under the co-chairmanship of Joint Secretary in charge of International Cooperation Division in the Ministry from Indian side and Dr. Pasquale D' Acunzi, President of ANICAV and Vice-President of Federalimentare (Italian Food Federation) from the Italian side. This Ministry, being the nodal Ministry also provides secretariat to the Working Group. The first session of the Working Group was held in Rome on 15th and 16th December, 1998. The two delegations agreed upon various projects for cooperation.

9

Consumer Cooperatives

Consumer Cooperatives are playing an important role in providing essential and other commodities to the public at reasonable prices. The presence of consumer cooperatives help in strengthening the distributive network of essential commodities, stabilising the price line, protection against artificial scarcity of goods by private traders, overcharging of prices, supply of substandard goods etc.

As a policy, the Government of India have been encouraging the development of consumer cooperatives so as to protect the interests of the common consumers. The consumer cooperatives are managed and controlled by the members through democratically elected bodies.

Structure of consumer cooperatives

The consumer cooperatives have a four-tier structure comprising primary consumer stores with branches functioning at the grass-root level, the wholesale/central consumer stores with their branches at district/taluka level, the State Consumer Cooperative Federations at the State level and the NCCF of India Ltd., at the national level. However, in the States located in the North East and in the smaller States/U.Ts. composite state level consumer-cum-marketing federation which deal with consumer articles also, are functioning. In the rural areas, the distribution of consumer goods is handled by the viable Large sized Agricultural Multi Purpose

Cooperative Societies (LAMPS) and/or Primary Agricultural Credit Societies (PACS) at the retail level.

Performance

Primary stores

In the urban areas the primary consumer cooperative stores play. a vital role in serving the consumers as also their members. Some of the consumer cooperative stores organised by the employees of large undertakings/ business houses are well managed ones. 'Me consumer stores organised by the employees of the Railways, Post & Telegraph, Port & Dock workers and by plantation employees are functioning very successfully. As per the information furnished by the Registrars of Cooperative. Societies of die States/U.Ts the total number of primary stores in the country is 25,570. Of theses, 12,478 were in profit, 7,415 in loss, 3,656 were either defunct or under liquidation while information regarding 2,021 stores is not available. The total paid-up share capital of these primary stores at the end of 1997-98 was Rs. 5562.64 lakhs of which State Government contribution was Rs. 1511.85 lakhs. The sales turnover of these primary stores was Rs. 137446.32 lakhs of which sales worth Rs. 87009.81 lakhs was due to controlled items. The total membership of these primary, stores was - 140.85 lakhs.

Wholesale/central stores

The total membership of such stores was 25.02 lakhs, comprising 2,28, lakhs individuals, 20.62 lakhs consumer cooperatives and 0. 16 other institutions/Govt. The total paid-up share capital of these stores as on 31.3.98 was Rs. 5685.32 lakhs, of which Govt. contribution was Rs.3436.02 lakhs. The total sales turnover achieved was Rs.184374.72 lakhs, which includes sales of controlled commodities amounting to Rs. 102751.22 lakhs. The setting up of big Department stores by consumer cooperatives have, however, not been able to keep pace with the rapid urbanisation and consequently the growing need of the urban population. There is a crying need for setting up of more such Department stores,

State federations

In so far as the states are concerned, the State Cooperative Consumers' Federations/State Cooperative Marketing-cum-Consumer Federations are the State level apex organisations. These State Federations provide supply support to the wholesale/central consumer stores. Some of the State Cooperative Consumer Federations have entered into the retail trade and have set up Department stores. In this connection, the names of Madhya Pradesh State Cooperative Federation, Assam State Co-operative Federation, Karnataka State Co-operative Federation and Goa State Cooperative Federations can be cited. The statement also indicates the total membership of these federations and their paid-up share capital. During the period, the total sales turnover of these federations was Rs. 131761.82 lakhs of which the retail sales was of Rs. 14913.73 lakhs.

The performance of the primary consumer cooperative stores, wholesale stores and the State Federations over a period of five years is, however, given at Annexure IV for a quick-comparison of the progress made by these tiers of the Consumer cooperative in the country.

Rural sector

In so far as the rural areas of the country are concerned, the viable LAMPS/PACS are involved in distribution of essential consumer articles at fair prices to the rural people especially those living in remote, inaccessible and hilly areas. It may be of special interest to note that with the success of cooperative movement in the dairy sector and in the processing sector like the cooperative sugar factories, Co-operative spinning mills etc. the entire rural economy of Maharashtra and Gujarat has undergone a tremendous change. This is reflected in the pattern and standard of living of the people of these states. This has resulted in opening of modem super markets/ department stores in the interior parts of these two States.

The National Cooperative Development Corporation (NCDC) has schemes for assisting the cooperatives for distribution of consumer articles in the rural areas. Under the scheme, the NCDC provides assistance to primary cooperative societies, wholesale consumer stores and branches of State Consumer Federations for undertaking distribution of consumer articles in the rural areas. Under this scheme assistance is provided to the cooperatives for purchase of furniture and fixtures for setting up of sales counter and purchase of transport vehicles. The total number of village societies for which financial assistance has been released by the NCDC, since the inception of the scheme till 31.3.98; is given at Annexure V. It can be seen from this statement that under this scheme, 50,463 village societies and 2816 of their branches have been assisted by the NCDC.

Physical achievement

The total retail sale handled by the Consumer Cooperatives in the urban and rural areas of the country during the year 1997-98 was about Rs. 4682.70 crores and Rs. 4448.50 crores; respectively. The retail sales to be handled by the Consumer Cooperatives in the urban and rural areas during 1998-99 is estimated to be about Rs. 5853.40 crores and Rs. 5560.62 crores respectively.

Role played by the consumer cooperatives in the Pds

The Consumer Cooperative Sector is playing an

important role in strengthening the public Distribution System (PDS) in the country. States like Madhya Pradesh and Tamil Nadu have almost all their fair price shops numbering 24,099 (upto December, 1997) and 23,622 out of 2489 1 (upto December, 1997) respectively, in the cooperative sector. As against a total no.of 4,49,469 fair price shops in the country upto December,1997, 94,124 i.e. 20.94% were being managed by the Consumer Cooperative Stores in the country.

Super bazar the cooperative stores limited, New Delhi

The Super Bazar, the Cooperative Store Limited started functioning from July, 1966 with one Super Market at Connaught Place, New Delhi. The store has now grown into one of the largest consumer cooperative store in the country with annual sales turnover of Rs. 126.80 (tentatively) during the year 1997-98. It has now 152 branches (4 of which are functioning in Noida area), 6 regional distribution centres and 18 drug outlets, of which 6 operate round-the clock. It also runs about 17 mobile van shops to cater to the needs of the far-flung areas including slum colonies. The Super Bazar, Delhi was the pioneer in introducing self-service system in its shops in the country. The membership of the Super Bazar, Delhi as on 31.3.1999 was Rs. 34,309. The paid-up share capital as on 31.3.1998 was 166.29 lakhs of which Govt. contribution was Rs. 126.99 lakhs. The Super Bazar, Delhi had been continuously earning profits since 1972-73 to 1995-96 and regularly paying dividend to its members including the Government. The Super Bazar had however sustained losses since 1996-97 and its sales had declined during 1997-98. Steps have, however, been initiated by the Super Bazar to increase its sales and profitability. The working results of the Super Bazar during the last three years were as under :-

Table

(Rs.in lakhs)

		1995-96 (Audited)	96-97 (Audited)	1997-98 (Tentative)
1.	Sales	13654.73	13847.85	12680.31
2.	Gross Profit	1157.94	1157.58	1066.80
3.	Net profit(+) Loss(-)	(+) 27.61	1157.58	1066.80

During the year the Super Bazar has undertaken distribution of onions, potatoes, palmolein and atta in the capital as their prices had shown sudden increase in the open market. The action taken by the Super Bazar, Delhi has helped in increasing the availability of these commodities in the open market thereby helping the consumers to get these commodities at reasonable prices. The role of the Super Bazar has been appreciated by the consumers in the capital.

National cooperative consumer federation of India limited, New Delhi

The National Cooperative Consumers' Federation of India Ltd.(NCCF) was registered in the year 1965 as an apex body of consumer cooperatives in the country. Its main objective is to provide supply support to its members, in particular, and other consumer cooperatives, in general, for distribution of consumer goods. It also renders technical and promotional guidance and assistance for increasing operational and managerial efficiency of the consumer cooperative stores. The commercial operations of the NCCF are undertaken through its headquarters at New Delhi and 15 branches and 8 liaison offices/depots located in different parts of the country. It has also set up two pulses processing units at Bhiwani and Nagpur.

As on 31.3.1998, the membership of the NCCF was 130. The membership of NCCF comprises the Government of India, the NCDC, the two National level federations i.e. National Agricultural Cooperative Marketing Federation of India Ltd. (NAFED) and National Cooperative Union of India (NCUI), State level federations and wholesale/primary stores. The paid-up share capital of the NCCF as on 31.3.1998 was Rs. 1143.34 lakhs, of which Govt.contribution was Rs. 855.24 lakhs.

NCCF is engaged in procurement and distribution of items in bulk like foodgrains, pulses, spices, textiles and various manufactured consumer goods. It has also made centralised arrangement for supply of selected consumer goods such as tea and iodised salt in consumer packs, toilet soap, match boxes and exercise note books in different States for distribution as additional item under PDS. In Delhi the Federation has continued to distribute the levy sugar in the areas allotted to it. In order to make available onions, potatoes and atta at rates prescribed by the Govt. of NCT of Delhi, NCCF has undertaken the distribution of these commodities to the consumers through its branches and mobile van shops. This has made a sobering effect on the retail prices of these items and availability in the open market in the Capital.

The sales achieved by the NCCF during the year 199798 was Rs. 255.77 crores with net profit of Rs. 59.82 law as against sales of Rs.207.29 crores with a net loss of Rs. 85.65 lakhs during 1996-97. This has reduced the accumulated losses of NCCF from Rs. 39.09 crores to Rs. 38.49 crores as on 31.3.1998.Forward markets commission-functions

The Forward Markets Commission (hereinafter referred to as the 'Commission') is a statutory body set up under the Forward Contracts (Regulation) Act, 1952 (hereinafter referred to as the 'Act'). The Commission functions under the administrative control of the Ministry of Food and Consumer Affairs, Department of Consumer Affairs, Government of India.

Under the Act , the Commission has following functions :-

(i) to advise the Central Government in respect of recognition or withdrawal of recognition of any association and other matters arising out of the administration of the Act;

(ii) to keep forward markets under observation and take appropriate action in relation to them;

(iii) to collect and publish information regarding trading conditions in respect of goods to which any of the provisions of the Act is made applicable including information regarding supply, demand and prices and to submit to Central Government periodical reports on the operation of this Act and on the working of the forward markets relating to such goods;

(iv) to make recommendations to improve the organisation and working of forward markets;

(v) to undertake inspection of the accounts of recognised associations and /or any members thereof;

(vi) to perform other duties prescribed by the Central Government.

The Commission thus is a statutory authority entrusted with regulatory functions under the Act. The Commission, at present, has a sanctioned strength of 4 members including the Chairman, out of which, 2 posts of members are vacant. It has its headquarters at Mumbai and a Regional Office at Calcutta. The Commission has 3 functional wings under it to carry out various tasks i.e.

the Commodity Division, the Enforcement Division and the Administration Division. The sanctioned strength of the office comprises 24 officers and 121 staff members.

Regulation of forward/futures trading

At present, futures trading is regulated through 15 recognised associations in 8 (eight) commodities viz.,

(i) Castorseed at Mumbai, Ahmedabad and Rajkot;

(ii) Pepper at Kochi; (both domestic and International)

(iii) Turmeric at Sangli;

(iv) Potatoes at Hapur, Kanpur and Agra.

(v) Gur at Hapur, Meerut, Muzaffarnagar, Bhatinda, Ludhiana, Gwalior, Agra, Kanpur and Delhi;

(vi) Hessian at Calcutta.

(vii) lute sacking at Calcutta. (viii) Cotton at Mumbai.

Besides, forward trading in the transferable specific delivery (T.S.D.) contracts and non-transferable specific delivery (N.T.S.D.) contracts are regulated in raw jute and jute goods under the auspices of one recognised Association at Calcutta. Likewise, trading in N.T.S.D. contracts continues to be regulated in cotton of different descriptions under the auspices of 8 recognised associations at Mumbai, Ahmedabad, Vadodara, Ujjain, Surat, Indore, Coimbatore and Guntur.

Recognised associations

There are 28 recognised Associations spread over in different parts of India. Of these presently 23 recognised Associations are functional.

Regulation of forward/futures trading by the commission

Forward/futures trading involves a passage of time between entering into a contract and its performance, making thereby the contracts susceptible to risks, uncertainties, etc. Hence the need for the regulatory functions to be exercised by the Commission.

After assessing the market situation and taking into account the recommendations made by the Board of Directors of the Exchange, the Commission prescribes various regulatory measures from time to time.

Resumption of futures trading in cotton

Following the decision of the Central Government to resume futures trading in cotton at one recognised Association viz., the East India Cotton Association, Mumbai, the said Association was directed to frame Bye-laws. The Association had accordingly framed their Bye-laws and the Commission had approved the same. The Commission had also, on 30.9.1998, granted permission to the said Association to commence trading in cotton futures in the December 1998, February 1999 and April 1999 deliveries, subject to regulatory measures such as limit on open position, payment of special margins on purchases and sales, limit on daily price variations maximum/minimum price etc. The mock trading in cotton in the Association had started on 12.10.98 and actual trading on December 5, 1998.

Registration of association

The Coffee Futures Exchange India Ltd., Bangalore had earlier submitted application for registration under section 14(B) of the Forward Contracts (Regulation) Act, 1952, for forward contracts in coffee. The Commission after examining the application and getting their bye-laws framed for conducting futures trading in coffee, has granted the Certificate of Registration on 13.2.1998 and the same is valid upto 31.3.2001. Presently trading in coffee futures is being organised on a trial basis at the Exchange.

The Soyabean Processors Association, Indore (SOPA) has been selected for futures contracts in soyabean, its oil & oilcake. It had earlier submitted an application for registration under section 14(B) of the Act. The SOPA has indicated a time frame for completing necessary preparation for commencing trading in soyabean, soyabean oil and oilcakes. This includes preparation of bye-laws, memorandum and articles of association, setting up of clearing house, etc. The preparations are expected to be completed by the end of August 1999. On completion of formalities, the Commission would consider granting registration to the said Association.

Price monitoring

The Commission also assists the Ministry of Food and Consumer Affairs in its work by undertaking an analysis of the prices of the essential commodities like foodgrains, pulses, edible oilseeds and oils, vanaspati, cotton, sugar and gur in the premier markets in the country. Besides this, the international price trends in many of the above commodities are also reviewed on a periodic basis. Furthermore, various aspects concerning the commodity economics of the above items are also reviewed and a regular feedback containing, inter-alia, the price trend and other developments in the domestic and overseas commodity markets are submitted to the Ministry. With a view to keep the Ministry informed of upto date position of commodity markets, the Commission continued the submission of the daily report to the Ministry, the data on wholesale and retail prices of various essential commodities, viz., rice, wheat, pulses, sugar, edible oils, vanaspati, onion, potato, tea, salt etc. in Mumbai.

Amendments to bye-laws and articles of associations

During the period under report extensive amendments to hedge trading bye laws relating to castorseed being traded at the Ahmedabad Seeds Merchants Association Ltd, Ahmedabad and the Rajkot Seeds Oil and Bullion Merchants Association Ltd., Rajkot were carried out. These amendments mainly related to the switching over from the system of weekly clearing to daily clearing and bye-laws relating to pay-in and pay-out etc.

International pepper futures contract at kochi

Following the setting up of International Commodity Exchange Division (IPSTA-ICE) at Kochi, the Commission granted permission for trading in the pepper futures contracts in the said Division for 9 deliveries during the period April 1998 to December 1998.

During the same period (April-December, 1998) the Commission also granted certificate of registration to three applicants for participation in the IPSTA-ICE.

Setting up of an international castor oil futures exchange at Mumbai

The Bombay Oilseeds and Oils Exchange Ltd., Mumbai has been granted recognition by the Central Government for trading in International Castoroil Futures through the International Castor' Oil Futures Exchange Division of the Association. The Exchange has framed draft set of Trading Bye-laws for facilitating such trading and draft set of Bye-laws for an independent Clearing House, a company proposed to be incorporated under the Companies Act by the name and style of the "Prime Commodities, Clearing Corporation of India Ltd." for registration and clearing the contracts traded through the Exchange. These Bye-laws are under discussion.

Inspection of associations

With a view to assess the performance of the commodity exchanges, to get first hand knowledge of the affairs of the exchanges, to understand any problem that may be faced by the commodity exchanges and to find the ways and means of improving their working, the Commission conducted~ inspection of 8 exchanges during the period from 1.4.1998 to 31.12.1998. The shortcomings noticed during the(inspections with reference to membership financial position administrative set up, improvement in the trading mechanism have been brought to their notice for rectification within time limits and are being pursued.

Forward markets bulletin and the commission's annual reports

The Commission also brings out a four monthly Bulletin entitled "Forward Markets Bulletin". The object of this bulletin is to present factual data relating to the working of the forward and futures markets in different commodities allowed in the country and to focus attention on the regulatory and other measures pertaining to these markets. Besides containing authoritative information c the regulation of forward/futures markets and renewal/grant of recognition to different associations, details of action against illegal forward/futures trading and options in goods and the training workshops organised by the Commission from time to time are also incorporated in the Bulletin. The 'Forward Markets Bulletin' also contains comprehensive reviews of different commodity markets in the country. The 'Forward Markets Bulletin' contains authoritative data on the ready and futures prices of different commodities at various centres. It also gives a gist of the regulatory provisions of the Act, as applied to the various commodities and texts of the Notifications issued under the Act by the Ministry of Food and Consumer Affairs.

The Forward Markets Bulletin, which is the only publication of its kind in the country, is subscribed to by Commodity Exchanges, Chambers of Commerce, Research Institutes and the trading community.

Besides bringing out the "Forward Markets Bulletin" the Commission also brings out its Annual Report. The Annual Report contains comprehensive review of the different commodity markets in the country, a gist of the regulatory measures prescribed for the forward/futures markets in the country as well as a wealth of statistical information pertaining to prices, trading activity and other allied matters relating to forward/futures markets

World bank grant

On a request made by the Government of India, the World Bank has approved a grant of 0.49 million dollars under IDF (Institutional Development Fund). This will be matched by a contribution of 0.079 million dollars by the Government of India. 'Me total project will thus cost US $ 0.569 million. The IDF Grant will be used to finance consultants' services, training, workshops and equipment to:-

(a) Strengthen the institutional capacity of the Forward Markets Commission (FMC), at the technical level, to fulfil its monitoring and regulatory functions adequately, develop a strategy for modernising the regulatory framework for futures markets, assist commodity exchanges in developing their own development strategies, and advise the Government of India about future policy directions in selected areas;

(b) Strengthen the institutional capacity of selected commodity exchanges at the technical level to develop a strategy for upgrading their trading bye-laws and clearing operations, and development capacity.

(c) Assist in the development of an effective market monitoring and surveillance mechanism to mitigate the risks of market manipulation.

In pursuance of these objectives the activities to be undertaken are:-

(a) a launching workshop.

(b) training of two types, (i) training abroad for officers of Government and FMC for a duration of one week; and (ii) training in India for officers of FMC, commodity exchanges and Trade etc.

(c) preparation of guidelines for improvements in several areas of trading, and monitoring and supervision of commodity markets both at the level of FMC and Commodity Exchanges. A total of 8 topics have been identified. These are identification and procurement of training material; development of training material; guidelines and bye-laws for clearing house operations; guidelines and bye-laws for brokerages; warehouse receipt system; development plan on market monitoring and surveillance system for commodity exchanges; market monitoring and surveillance system for FMC; development of software for market monitoring and surveillance system.

(d) acquisition of training equipment for FMC; and

(e) visit to commodity ' exchanges and regulatory authorities outside India by office bearers of commodity exchanges and FMC/Government officials.

The programme will cover only selected Commodity Exchanges. The duration-of the programme is 18 months from June 98 onwards.

Accordingly, a workshop on Commodities Futures Markets was organised at New Delhi on the 17th and 18th September 1998 in collaboration with the World Bank. The purpose of the workshop was to create awareness on futures trading, expose the participants to latest developments in the field and to prepare the commodity exchanges for strengthening their systems and procedure to be able to organise futures trading in large number of commodities in an organised manner. The response was overwhelming. More than 250 participants took part in the workshop. The Minister of State for Food and Consumer Affairs Shri Satpal Singh Yadav inaugurated the workshop.

A team comprising officials from the Ministry of Food and Consumer Affairs, Forward Markets Commission and representatives of selected commodity exchanges visited the major futures exchanges in Chicago and New York which are organising futures trading in commodities, foreign currencies, stock indices and securities. The visit was undertaken in October-November, 98. The officials of the Ministry and Forward Markets Commission attended a Training Seminar conducted by the regulatory body of USA viz., the Commodity Futures Trading Commission in October, 1998.

Enforcement activities of the commission

The forward/futures contracts are prohibited or suspended in a number of commodities, including many essential commodities such as foodgrains, pulses, edible oilseeds and oils. Consequently entering into forward/ futures contracts in these commodities is an offence attracting the penal provisions of the Act. Besides, 'options' in goods are totally prohibited under the Act.

The powers to search, seize, investigate and prosecute in respect of offences under the Act are not vested with the Commission or its officers. These powers are vested with the police authorities of the concerned State/Union Territories. The Enforcement Division of the

Commission, however, performs a crucial role by assisting the police in a number of ways. The functions of this Division include:-

(i) collection, collation and development of information pertaining to illegal forward/futures trading and options in goods.

(ii) communication of this information to the police, requesting them to carry out enforcement action, wherever necessary.

(iii) assistance to the police at the time of raids by accompanying them and helping them in selecting and seizing the incriminating documents.

(iv) scrutiny of documents seized by the police involving decoding of complicated entries concerning the technicalities of forward trading, which in turn involves translation/transliteration of the documents on the one hand and interpretation and collation on these entries, in the light of the relevant legal provisions, on the other.

(v) officers of this Division appear as expert witnesses on behalf of the prosecution in different Courts of Law, and

(vi) examination of court judgement with a view of exploring and suggesting the possibility of appeal to the prosecution.

The police authorities in different parts of the country carried out 33 raids for alleged illegal forward trading in banned commodities and options in goods during the period April-December, 1998.

During the period April-December, 1998, 161 -documents were scrutinised and 14 scrutiny reports containing the expert opinion of the Commission regarding the nature of evidence found in the documents were sent to the police authorities.

During the period April-December, 1998, no information was received regarding prosecution launched and no convictions were secured during the period. Neither April 98 were there any case of acquittal/ discharge. May 98

The details of raids reported, scrutiny reports sent and June 98 prosecution launched during period April-December, 1998, July 98 is given at Annex-1.

The police officers at the operational level of Inspectors and Sub- Inspectors are trained periodically so as to acquaint them with the nature of offence under the Act, the modus operandi employed by the offenders, including the adroit changes made therein from time to time and the basic legal provisions pertaining to the nature of the different forms of forward contracts under the Act. Police prosecutors are also familiarised with the technicalities of the subject so as to enable them to perform their duties effectively. In addition, Jan. 9 workshops on Forward Trading for senior police officers and Judicial Magistrates are organised so as to enable them Feb. to appreciate the gravity of offence under the Act which are basically in the nature of economic offences.

During the period April-December, 1998, 10 training courses for police officers, and prosecutors were conducted one each at Navi Mumbai, Hyderabad, Sholapur, Nasik, Coimbatore, Bhopal, Lucknow, Thane, Madhuban and Jaipur. A total number of 358 police officers and police prosecutors were trained during this period.

The Bureau of Indian Standards, the National Standards Body of India, became functional as a statutory body under the Bureau of Indian Standards Act, 1986 with effect from I April 1987 taking over the staff, assets and liabilities of the Indian Standards Institution established in 1947. The Bureau has been successfully promoting and nurturing the standardization movement in the country. During 1998-99, BIS has made all round progress in its various activities relating to standardization, certification (both product and quality systems).

Standards formulation

The BIS is formulating need-based Indian Standards in line with the national priorities as a time-bound programme. The Bureau has taken a decision to harmonize national standards with regional and international standards in order to facilitate adoption of international standards by all segments of business and industry. Till date, more than 3390 Indian standards have been harmonised with international standards.

Table
Progress of standards formulation

Sl. No.	*Activities*	*Progress during* 1997-98	*Apr-Dec. 98*
1.	New and revised standards formulated	298	205
2.	Draft Standards Finalised and widely circulated	308	236
3.	Standards in force	17113*	17184*
4.	Review of standards	3212	1556

Promotional activities

State level committees on standardization and quality systems

State Level Committees on Standardization and Quality

Systems have been established in 25 States and Union Territories for strengthening standardization, quality systems and testing facilities in the States. The State Governments through these committees play an important role in upgradation of quality of products manufactured in the respective states by advising the manufacturers to implement standards and propagating the concept of giving preference to ISI marked goods for purchase by Government Departments/Organisations.

World standards day

To commemorate the foundation of International Organization for Standardization (ISO), the World Standards Day was celebrated all over the world on 14 October 1998. To mark the occassion, BIS organized seminars, talks, lectures and exhibitions throughout the country on the theme "Standards in Daily Life". The seminar at New Delhi was inaugurated by the Secretary, Department of Consumer Affairs, Ministry of Food & Consumer Affairs.

Rajiv Gandhi national quality award

The Rajiv Gandhi National Quality Award was instituted by the BIS in 1991 with a view to encourage Indian manufacturing and service organisations to strive for excellence and giving special recognition to those who are considered to be the leaders of quality movement in India. The Award has been named after the late Prime Minister, Shri Rajiv Gandhi, recognising the new thrust he had given to the quality movement in India so that it could move into the 21st century with pride.

Certification

Product Certification - The BIS has been operating product certification scheme for more than four decades. Under the Scheme, 1012 new licences were granted during April to Dec. 1998, bringing the number of operative licences to 13065. Thirteen new products were covered during this period, the important products being cycle rubber tubes, processed cereal based complimentary foods for infants, grading of viscose rayon cut staple fibres (regular), forged brass gate, globe and check valves for water works purposes, direct action hand pumps, coffers, functional requirements for stand post type water monitor for fire fighting, dust-pressed ceramic tiles, spectrometer (student type), glass fibre reinforced plastics (GRP) pipes, joints & fittings for use for sewerage, industrial waste & water (other than potable), Ethephon solution and cash boxes. The progress of certification marks activity is summerised in Table 2.

Table

Progress of certification marks activities

Sl No.	Activities	Progress during 1997-98	Apr-Dec.98
1.	Applications received	2222	1418
2.	Licences granted	1504	1012
3.	Licences cancelled/expired	1089	978
4.	Preliminary inspections done	1879	1291
5.	Periodic inspections done	16961	13743
6.	Market samples drawn	10489	5620
7.	Samples tested in BIS labs	27712	19720

Quality System Certification - The BIS Quality System Certification Scheme also made steady progress with grant of 67 licences for ISO 9000 certification during April to December 1998, bringing the number of licences to 414.

The Quality System Certification Scheme has already been accredited by Raad voor Accreditatie (RvA) of Netherland (a body of international repute;) for 18 technology sectors. An application has been made to RvA, for covering a few more sectors like Hotel and Restaurant Industries.

Environmental management system certification

The BIS has adopted the ISO standards pertaining to Environmental Management Systems (ISO 14000 series). These standards specify requirements for an Environmental Management System to enable an organisation to formulate a policy and objectives taking into account legislative requirements and information about significant environmental impacts.

The BIS has launched the Environmental Management System Certification Scheme for industrial units which are conscious of the need for maintaining a greener environment. The scheme will have a bench mark for compliance with environment laws applicable in the country with -emphasis on continuous improvement. A number of officers have been trained in this field and a new department namely the Environmental Management Systems Department has been set up for certification of Environmental Management Systems. Under the scheme, a licence to a cement unit has been granted.

Enforcement

In its endeavour to sustain the popularity of its standard mark, the BIS has strengthened its enforcement activities. It organized enforcement-cum-consumer awareness drives throughout the country to educate the common consumer -about their rights, benefits of purchasing certified goods and different forms of misuse of its Standard Mark normally adopted by manufacturers/ suppliers, so that the consumer can distinguish between a genuine mark and forged one. Fifteen raids were also organised with the help of State Governments for misuse of ISI mark during this period.

Laboratories

The BIS, with a network of eight laboratories spread all over the country, supports the product certification scheme by ascertaining the conformity of certified products against the relevant Indian standards. The number of samples tested during the year 1997-98 and April to December 1998 in these laboratories are given in Table 2.

The BIS laboratories also undertake work related to quality evaluation, validation of test methods, calibration, development/modification of test equipments etc. BIS laboratories also organise training programmes on product testing for personnel both from the BIS and the industry.

The BIS is augmenting and modernising its testing laboratories to upgrade them to the international level. BIS Central laboratory and Western Regional laboratory have got accreditation for its mechanical, electrical and chemical testing facilities from the National Accreditation Board for Testing and Calibration Laboratories (NABL) of the Department of Science & Technology, Government of India under its NABL scheme. In addition to these, other Regional Laboratories are preparing for obtaining accreditation from NABL, Department of Science and Technology. Recently Eastern Regional Laboratory at Calcutta has received accredition from NABL, Deptt. of Science and Technology.

Technical information services

The BIS is providing information about standards, technical regulations and quality systems through its Technical Information Services Centre. A number of bibliographies were provided to the users from the computer data base on world wide standards. The BIS also brings out information bulletins regularly. Progress in these activities is given in Table 3.

Table

Progress on Technical Service

Sl	*Activities No.*	*Progress during* 1997-98	*Apr.-Dec. 98*
1.	Technical queries attended to	7016	5994
2.	Publications loaned	87634	27784
3.	Publications added	11297	10016
4.	Library Membership	1461	906
5.	Bibliography	14	6

Central enquiry point under wto

The World Trade Organization (WTO), Agreement on Technical Barriers to Trade- popularly known as WTO Standards Code was brought out in 1979 to eliminate technical barriers to international trade. The BIS has been nominated by the Government of India to function as the National Central Enquiry Point. The Enquiry Point collects information on national standards, technical regulations and certification systems in India and also answers queries about these from other countries. The Enquiry Point issues notifications to the AFM Secretariat (Geneva) on new standards/amendments/ revisions etc. issued by BIS for benefit of member countries.

Training programmes

The BIS organised training programmes for industry personnel in the field of Statistical Quality Control, quality system documentation, quality system auditing, enhancing management representatives skills, awareness programme on standardization and quality system, product testing etc.

During the year training programmes for BIS employees were organised in the field of environment management system, computers, referesher course in certification, quality system, standardization, style manual, increasing efficiency etc. During this period 107 BIS employees received training.

International activities

The International Electrotechnical Commission (IEC) founded in 1906 is composed of National Committees, of which there are 52 at present, representing all the industrial countries in the world. IEC has served the electrical, electronics and telecommunication industries by developing international standards to promote quality, safety, performance, reproducibility and environmental compatibility of materials, products and systems. The 62nd General Meeting of IEC was held in Houston, USA from 12 to 17 October 1998. A delegation, with senior officials from BIS represented India in the meeting.

The BIS also continued to actively participate in the various technical and policy making committees of International Organisation for Standardization (ISO).

Revenue mobilisation

BIS derives its income mainly from product certification, quality system certification and sale of Indian standards. The income from these resources during April Dec. 1998 was 344.08 million-rupees.

Reservation for scheduled castes/scheduled tribes and hnadicapped persons

The staff strength of the BIS was 2197 as on December 1998. Group-wise representation of SC/ST and physically handicapped persons are indicated below:-

Group	*SC*	*ST*	*OBC*	*Handicapped*
A	54	8	-	1
B	31	1	1	-

D	154	18	4	11
54	147	22	-	8

Publicity

The BIS continued to publicise its different activities through sustained use of mass media communication. The interviews and talks of BIS officials were telecast and broadcast from various stations of the all-India Radio, Doordarshan Kendras and private TV Channels. The BIS officials also participated in various discussions, interviews and in different fora on matters relating to its activities.

Monthly and quarterly bulletins and news letters such as Standards India, EC Norm Scan, 'IT - Standards' etc. were brought out regularly to keep the concerned. interests informed on the developments in standardisation at national and international level in specific fields. A Bulletin entitled "BIS and CONSUMER" was also issued in April 1998, keeping in view the Consumer welfare.

BIS participated in a number of exhibitions fairs in order to increase awareness among the consumers about the benefits of standardization. It also organised conferences and seminars all over the country to highlight the work undertaken in the field of standardization and quality systems.

Progressive use of hind in BIS work

Various steps have been undertaken for implementation of the provisions of the Official Languages Act in the day to day work. A number of articles, general orders, office notes, press communiques and covering letters of draft Indian Standards and amendments were issued in Hindi.

'Hindi Pakhwara' was celebrated during 14-25 Sept 1998, by organising various competitions in typing, stenography, telegrams and technical articles in Hindi. Hindi exhibition was also organised during the Pakhwara wherein the BIS personnel participated with great enthusiasm. Hindi Day was celebrated in different regional and branch offices of BIS.

10

Regulation of Weights and Measures

The Weights and Measures laws in the country are enforced through the Standards of Weights and Measures Act,1976 and the Standards of Weights and Measures (Enforcement) Act,1985. Through these legislations, the Government ensures that all weights and measures used in trade, transaction, industrial production or protection of human health and safety are accurate and reliable so that users are guaranteed accuracy of their performance. This in turn enables the consumers to get the right quality/quantity of goods for which they are paying. With the rapid development in the field of science and technology coupled with the liberalization policy being pursued by the Government, a number of state-of-the-art weighing and measuring instruments are finding their way into the Indian market. To ensure quality control and uniformity in these new types of weights and measures, their specifications also need to be updated. The Department has already set in motion the process of adopting these new specifications in the General Rules, in alignment with the recommendations made by the International Organization of Legal Metrology (O1ML). In this direction, the Rules were amended revising the specifications of "non-automatic weighing instruments"in line with the international recommendation. Adoption of the new specifications would help the Indian industries to compete in the -international market.

The weights and measures regulations in India also regulate the sale of commodities in pre-packed form. The Standards of Weights and Measures (Packaged Commodities) Rules,1977 require mandatory declaration of some basic information on packages to safeguard the interests of consumers. The Rules also require importers to provide certain basic declarations on the imported packages, similar to those for indigenous packages.

Indian institute of legal metrology, Ranchi

To impart training to the enforcement officials of Weights & Measures, the Institute has been running a fourmonth basic training course. The Institute has been conducting training seminars on 'Consumer Protection' for the non-judicial members of the State Commissions, District Fora set up under the Consumer Protection Act. Besides, the Institute propose to conduct a six- month integrated training program for officers from developing countries. The Institute, in addition, conducts workshops and seminars of shorter durations on specific topics' to update the knowledge of the enforcement officers on the latest developments in the field of Legal Metrology. On an average, the Institute trains about 200 personnel every year.

Regional reference standards laboratories

The Central Government has established 3 Regional Reference Standards Laboratories (RRSL) at Ahmedabad, Bhubaneswar and Bangalore. These RRSLs serve as a link in disseminating the values of national standards of weights and measures down to the commercial level. During the 9th Five Year Plan period, the Ministry has undertaken to implement three new schemes namely, establishing a RRSL for the northern region of the country, a RRSL for the north eastern region and construction of a laboratory building for RRSL at Bhubaneswar. The existing laboratories at Ahmedabad and Bangalore are also being modernized to meet the requirements of the industry.

Apart from the statutory obligation of verification of legal standards of the States and conducting model approval tests of weights or measures, these laboratories have been rendering metrological services to industries by under taking calibration of their weighing and measuring instruments. Each laboratory on an average provides calibration service to about 100 industries in the region.

Reservation of scheduled caste and scheduled tribes

The instructions issued by the Department of Personnel and Training from time to time regarding representation of Scheduled Castes/Scheduled Tribes in direct recruitment and promotion to various grade and services were followed.

The number of persons belonging to Scheduled Castes, Scheduled Tribes, Other Backward Classes, Physically Handicapped and Ex-servicemen employed in the Department and its offices are indicated below:-

(as on 10.2.1999)

Category	*Group A*	*Group B*	*Group C*		*Group*
	Gazetted		*Non-Gazetted*		
Scheduled Castes	11	2	15	21	32
Scheduled Tribes	2	-	2	9	13
Other Backward Classes	1	-	1	6	16
Physically Handicapped					
VH	-	-	0	-	I
HH	-	-	-	-	0
OH	1	-	1	4	-
Ex-servicemen	I	-	-	2	3
General	39	20	43	101	51
Total:	55	22	62	143	116

Progressive use of Hindi

During the year, appropriate action was taken to ensure implementation of the provision of the Official Languages Act and the Rules framed thereunder.

The Annual Programme for the year 1998-99 for implementation of the Official Language Policy of the Union, issued by the Department of Official Language as well as orders issued by them from time to time in this regard were circulated in the Department and to all the attached/ subordinate offices/corporations etc. for compliance. Progress made in this regard was reviewed through the quarterly reports received from them.

Regular meetings of the official language implementation committee, set up in the Department to review the progress made in implementation of Official Language policy in the Department as well as in its attached/ subordinate offices etc. were held during the year.

For ensuring compliance with the provisions of the Official Languages Act, 1963 and rules framed thereunder, check points have been set up in the Department. Effective steps were taken for the adherence to these check points.

Steps were taken to ensure progressive use of Hindi for correspondence with Hindi speaking States and Union Territories.

Employees not trained in Hindi, Hindi stenography and Hindi typing were nominated for training in the respective fields.

The attached/subordinate offices under the Department wherein 80% or more than 80% of staff (except Group V) have working knowledge in Hindi have been notified in the Gazette of India as required in Rule

10(4) of the Official Languages (use for official purposes of the Union) Rules 1976. Orders to make all correspondence in Hindi under rule 8(4) of the said Rules have also been issued by the Department and the offices so notified under rule 10(4).

Entries were invited for the block year 1994-96 under the scheme of award for original writing in Hindi and after the evaluation of entries, the prizes were announced.

'Me scheme for awarding cash prizes to Central Govt. Employees for noting and drafting in Hindi continued to be implemented during the year.

Special incentive for doing Hindi typing in addition to English typing continued to be given to employees of the Department.

The quarterly magazine "Upabhokta Jagaran" meant for creating awareness among the consumers for their rights continued to be brought out both in Hindi and English.

To impart training in noting and drafting in Hindi, workshops were organised in the Department.

Continuous efforts art being made to encourage progressive use of Hindi in official work not only in the Department but also in the attached and subordinate offices. Inspections were conducted from time to time to watch the progress in this regard. Hindi Books, News papers, Magazines and journals were purchased regularly for the library of the Department.

The Department organised "HINDI FORTNIGHT" during 1-15 September, 1998. During this period, competitions in essay, noting/drafting in Hindi, Hindi stenography, Hindi typewriting and the quantum of work done in Hindi were organised and prizes/ certificates were distributed to the winners in a function.